HIRING COSTS AND STRATEGIES
THE AMA REPORT

AMACOM BRIEFINGS & SURVEYS

Don Lee Bohl, Editor
Eric Rolfe Greenberg, Project Director
Anne Skagen, Associate Editor
John Aberth, Editorial Associate

American Management Association
135 West 50th Street
New York, N.Y. 10020

©1986 AMA Membership Publications Division, American Management Association, New York. All rights reserved. Printed in the United States of America.

This publication has been distributed to individuals enrolled in the Human Resources Division of the American Management Association.

This publication may not be reproduced, stored in a retrieval system, or transmitted in whole or in part, in any form or by any means, electronic, mechanical, photocopying, recording, or otherwise, without the prior written permission of AMA Membership Publications Division, 135 West 50th Street, New York, New York 10020.

First Printing
ISBN 0-8144-3153-4

Price: $85 to AMA members, $100 to non-members.

CONTENTS

	Page
Highlights and Conclusions	1
Introduction	3
SECTION I. AN OVERVIEW OF HIRING COSTS AND STRATEGIES	5
The AMA Questionnaire	5
1. Recruiting Strategies	11
2. Advertising Costs and Practices	24
3. Recruiter Salaries and Work Loads	27
4. Travel, Lodging and Entertainment	29
5. Screening Interviews and Referrals	32
6. Close-Up On Testing: Its Future in the Workplace	34
7. Relocation Expenses	41
8. Other Direct Costs	43
9. Chargeback Policies	45
10. Filling the Position: The Time Factor	46
11. Filling the Position: The First Selection Factor	47
12. Up-To-Speed Expectations	49
SECTION II. HIRING COSTS: THE KEY INDICATORS	51
General Manager, $+80K	55
Senior Financial Officer, $60-$65K	57
MIS Director, $55-60K	59
Purchasing Director, $47-$50K	61
Sales Manager, $42-45K	63
Plant Personnel Manager, $40-$42K	65
Product Manager, $35-$38K	67

HIRING COSTS AND STRATEGIES: THE AMA REPORT

	Page
Market Research Manager, $32-35K	69
Telemarketing Manager, $30-32K	71
Computer Programmer, $26-28K	73
Human Resource Specialist, $26-$28K	75
Staff Accountant, $24-26K	77

SECTION III. THE RESPONDENT PROFILE   79

LIST OF TABLES

		Page
Table 1.	Number of Approaches Used in Recruiting	11
Table 2.	Preferred Approaches Used In Recruiting	13
Table 3.	Respondents Who Would Check Files of Previous Applicants	14
Table 4.	Respondents Who Would Post Listings for In-House Applicants	15
Table 5.	Respondents Who Would Use an In-House Referral System	16
Table 6.	Private Employment Agency/Executive Search Firm Options	17
Table 7.	Respondents Who Would Use A Private Employment Agency	18
Table 8.	Respondents Who Would Use An Executive Search Firm	18
Table 9.	Employment Agency/Search Firm Fees	19
Table 10.	Respondents Who Would Use a Public Employment Bureau	20
Table 11.	Respondents Who Would Use a College Recruitment Program	21
Table 12.	Respondents Who Would Use an On-Site/Off-Site Open House	22
Table 13.	Media Choices in Advertising Open Positions	24
Table 14.	Annual Salary of Recruiter Assigned to Fill Open Position	27
Table 15.	Number of Open Assignments Recruiters Carry Concurrently	28
Table 16.	Budgets for Candidate Travel, Lodging & Entertainment	30
Table 17.	Budgets for Recruiter Travel, Lodging & Entertainment	31
Table 18.	Initial Screening Interviews/Referrals to Supervisor	32
Table 19.	Maximum Budgeted Amounts for Relocation Expenses	41
Table 20.	Respondents Who Budget For Relocation Expenses/ Respondents Who Set No Maximum Amounts	42
Table 21.	Budget Allocations For Other Direct Costs	44
Table 22.	Recruitment Costs Charged Back To Departments	45
Table 23.	Number of Weeks To Fill Position	46
Table 24.	Prospects of Adequately Filling Position with First Selection	48
Table 25.	Up-To-Speed Expectations	49

HIRING COSTS AND STRATEGIES: THE AMA REPORT

		Page
Table 26.	All Positions: Labor Cost of Hire	51
Table 27.	General Manager: National and Regional Costs	54
Table 28.	General Manager: Labor Cost of Hire	55
Table 29.	Senior Financial Officer: National and Regional Costs	56
Table 30.	Senior Financial Officer: Labor Cost of Hire	57
Table 31.	MIS Director: National and Regional Costs	58
Table 32.	MIS Director: Labor Cost of Hire	59
Table 33.	Purchasing Director: National and Regional Costs	60
Table 34.	Purchasing Director: Labor Cost of Hire	61
Table 35.	Sales Manager: National and Regional Costs	62
Table 36.	Sales Manager: Labor Cost of Hire	63
Table 37.	Plant Personnel Manager: National and Regional Costs	64
Table 38.	Plant Personnel Manager: Labor Cost of Hire	65
Table 39.	Product Manager: National and Regional Costs	66
Table 40.	Product Manager: Labor Cost of Hire	67
Table 41.	Market Research Manager: National and Regional Costs	68
Table 42.	Market Research Manager: Labor Cost of Hire	69
Table 43.	Telemarketing Manager: National and Regional Costs	70
Table 44.	Telemarketing Manager: Labor Cost of Hire	71
Table 45.	Computer Programmer: National and Regional Costs	72
Table 46.	Computer Programmer: Labor Cost of Hire	73
Table 47.	Human Resources Specialist: National and Regional Costs	74
Table 48.	Human Resources Specialist: Labor Cost of Hire	75
Table 49.	Staff Accountant: National and Regional Costs	76
Table 50.	Staff Accountant: Labor Cost of Hire	77
Table 51.	Respondents by Economic Activity	79
Table 52.	Respondents by Geographic Distribution/Organizational Size	80
Table 53.	Respondents by Geographic Distribution/Economic Activity	80
Table 54.	Respondents per Position Description by Size/Turnover Rate	81

HIGHLIGHTS AND CONCLUSIONS

The hiring process presents the human resources manager with a variety of options. Their exercise can result in an extraordinary range of costs-per-hire -- from less than a thousand dollars for local advertising and departmental charges to over a hundred thousand dollars for search firm fees, relocation expenses, and travel, lodging, and entertainment for both candidates and recruiters.

Seeking outside assistance increases costs enormously. Aware of that, fewer than half of the human resources managers polled would use an employment agency or executive search firm to fill most management positions. Where they are used, search firms are preferred for positions paying $50,000 or more, agencies for posts paying from $25,000 to $45,000. Though fees vary regionally and according to the position to be filled, the largest share of companies expect to pay 25 per cent of annual salary to an employment agency, and 30 per cent to an executive search firm.

To fill most managerial positions, human resources managers opt for low-cost techniques that confine the search to in-house candidates and previous job applicants. These programs are frequently combined with an in-house referral system that offers awards, typically ranging from $200 to $500, for recommending a successful candidate.

One in five respondents contact public and community employment bureaus in their recruitment process; the percentage is higher at the lower end of the managerial salary scale. A college recruitment program is utilized by a third of our respondents to fill entry-level positions. Open houses, job fairs, professional associations and personal networking are infrequent search tools. Generally, the techniques that cost the least are most favored.

Advertising is frequently the single greatest expenditure in the hiring process, especially local advertising, where budgets typically run well over $1,000 for higher salaried posts and nearly as much for jobs paying $25,000 to $35,000. Regional and national ad budgets are generally higher, but respondents use those media far less frequently; the same is true of advertising in trade and professional journals. The standard is to advertise locally and in one other category -- regional, national, or trade/professional -- with the choice determined by the special needs of the organization and the distribution of qualified candidates.

HIRING COSTS AND STRATEGIES: THE AMA REPORT

Recruiter salaries average $37,200 in large companies (those with more than $500 million in annual sales), $33,100 in mid-sized firms ($50 million to $500 million), and $32,000 in small companies (under $50 million in annual sales or budget). Large firms assign recruiters greater case loads, frequently twice that of a small company recruiter; in so doing they keep the labor cost of recruiting below that of the small firms, despite the higher salaries they pay.

Travel, lodging and entertainment for both candidates and recruiters are significant expenses which vary according to the salary level of the position to be filled. Expenditures of $2,500 on candidates for high salaried posts are not unusual, nor are $1,250 budgets for recruiter travel.

Typically, human resources managers will interview eight to ten candidates for an open position, referring three or four on to the position supervisor for further consideration. These numbers are remarkably consistent, whatever the size of the organization or its annual rate of turnover for management positions.

Testing of whatever sort -- job skill, psychological, behavioral, or polygraph -- is infrequently applied. Many respondents doubt that such tests can be validated to conform to EEOC requirements.

Relocation costs, if offered to candidates, increase expenses more than any other single factor in the hiring process. Charges in excess of $25,000 are not unusual, and some large companies involve themselves in house purchases, mortgage assumptions, and other extraordinary expenses. Naturally, organizations take on such burdens for high-salaried talent; few offer help of any kind to entry-level managers.

Two-thirds of human resources departments charge advertising costs back to the departments where positions are open; half charge back agency fees, relocation costs, and candidate T, L & E expenses. Most absorb recruiter expenses and interview time within departmental budgets.

All these costs must be borne again if the selection does not work out successfully; despite this, human resources managers are not overly optimistic that the first chosen proves right. Only a third rated as "excellent" their prospects of adequately filling the position with their first choice. Most expect the new hire to be up to speed after six months on the job, although one in five consider that it will take longer -- up to one year.

Important regional variations exist in all these costs. Advertising rates on the East and West Coasts and in the large midwestern cities affect ad budgets. Prospects of filling jobs locally affect relocation budgets and travel and lodging costs for both candidates and recruiters. Costs are also a function of organizational size and turnover rates, with shifting effects in different categories.

INTRODUCTION

"There are three kinds of lies," Benjamin Disraeli observed on a famous occasion, "lies, damned lies, and statistics." Certainly statistics can easily misinform or only partially inform the seeker of knowledge; numbers are of all things exact, but what one makes of the numbers is often inexact.

There is a classic method of determining hiring costs. At year's end one adds up the entire amount spent in the hiring process, divides by the number of people hired, and arrives at a simple result: the arithmetic cost-per-hire. This statistic does not lie, and it has its budgetary uses. But the figure obscures far more than it reveals.

For the human resources manager, the hiring process is one of constant choice, and the ultimate choice -- the person to hire for the job -- is but the last in a long series. Shall I fill this position in-house or on the outside? Shall I use an employment agency? An executive search firm? A public employment bureau? Shall I advertise for the post? Locally? Nationally? In trade publications? Need I send a recruiter on the road to interview and evaluate candidates -- or should I invite candidates to the workplace at corporate expense?

Of course, the answer to each of these questions is made on a case-by-case basis; that is the recruiter's job. And, similarly, the answer to each question will ultimately determine the cost of hiring a particular individual to fill a particular position. We see immediately, then, how uninformative is the classic cost-per-hire formula to the recruiter who must fill a particular position and who must forecast the cost of doing so. The classic formula does not differentiate between the cost of hiring a new general manager or a new pool typist. To obtain more specific information, a different approach was required.

It was to collect such data, <u>case-by-case</u> data, that AMA's Membership Briefings and Surveys staff designed and prepared this Report on Hiring Costs and Strategies, to serve as guidelines and benchmarks for the human resources community.

First, we prepared a series of very brief position descriptions and salary levels for a dozen fairly typical management jobs. Then, in effect, we asked respondents to tell us the choices they would make in recruiting for these positions, and the costs that would

HIRING COSTS AND STRATEGIES: THE AMA REPORT

result. We also collected data on key result measurements -- the speed with which a position is filled, the time by which the new hire is "up to speed," and the likelihood that the person hired will prove right for the job.

In analyzing the data we paid particular attention to the size and geographic location of our respondent organizations to discover if these variables had a significant effect on hiring costs. We also studied the numbers to see if companies with high turnover rates among managers pursued different strategies from organizations with more stable work forces.

This report is organized into three sections.

In Section I, we take the readers through the AMA questionnaire and provide a general overview of our findings on strategies and costs. Our concern is as much with choices as costs. We are interested in knowing how human resources managers exercise the many options they hold in the hiring process.

In Section II, we take a closer look at the findings for each of the twelve position descriptions we developed for the study, with particular attention to regional breakouts of the data. Here we concentrate on costs, giving the average expenditures for those who have opted for agencies or search firms; referral awards; print advertising; travel, lodging and entertainment for both candidates and recruiters; and relocation.

In Section III, we present a respondent profile in charts that readers may study to perform their own analyses.

SECTION I

AN OVERVIEW OF HIRING COSTS AND STRATEGIES

The AMA Questionnaire

There were two forms of the AMA Hiring Costs and Strategies questionnaire. The questions on both forms were identical; the hypothetical position descriptions above the questions were not.

Form A had six position descriptions, set in three matched pairs; respondents could choose one position in each matched pair and answer the questions as they pertained to that choice. Form B had six additional position descriptions, likewise set in three matched pairs; here again respondents chose one from each matched pair and answered the questions accordingly.

While the survey sought information on hiring costs and strategies for the particular positions listed, we may draw useful conclusions from from the total database for all twelve positions. In this section, a general overview of findings, we shall do so.

Before proceeding, however, let us look at the position descriptions themselves, as they were matched together in Forms A and B of the questionnaire.

Form A featured these positions:

> **GENERAL MANAGER**, responsible for all aspects of product line from materials procurement to sales/marketing; reports directly to Executive V.P./COO. Minimum 18 years experience in managerial position, 8 years in senior management. Salary range: $80,000+.

matched with:

> **MIS DIRECTOR**, responsible for systems programming, telecommunications, hardware and software evaluation and purchasing; budgetary responsibilities, capacity planning. Minimum 10 years experience; advanced degree in computer sciences or related field. Salary range: $55-60,000.

HIRING COSTS AND STRATEGIES: THE AMA REPORT

MARKET RESEARCH MANAGER, responsible for supervising and analyzing research projects for existing and new products and services, designing research instruments, conducting field work and focus groups. Degree (MBA preferred); 3 to 5 years experience. Salary range: $32-35,000.

matched with:

PRODUCT MANAGER, responsible for supervision of production line work teams, quality control, work assignments; degree in engineering or related field; minimum 8 years experience. Salary range: $35-38,000.

HUMAN RESOURCES SPECIALIST, responsible for recruitment, job placement, career counseling and group counseling. Minimum 2 to 3 years experience; master's degree in personnel or related field. Salary range: $26-28,000.

matched with:

STAFF ACCOUNTANT, responsible for monthly closings, journal entry preparation, account analysis and statement preparation, occasional special project assignments. Master's degree in accounting; some experience preferred but not essential (possible entry-level position). Salary range: $24-26,000.

Form B of the questionnaire featured these positions:

SENIOR FINANCIAL OFFICER, responsible for financing, budgeting and related activities; master's degree in accounting or business administration; minimum 10 years experience. Salary range: $60-65,000.

matched with:

DIRECTOR OF PURCHASING, responsible for implementing new inventory procedures, inventory reduction, vendor relations, coordination with manufacturing and marketing departments; MBA or similar degree; minimum 10 years experience. Salary range: $47-50,000.

SALES MANAGER, responsible for directing national sales force, determining staff needs, evaluating distribution channels, developing accounts and forecasting sales. BA in business, marketing, or related field; minimum 5 years sales experience, 3 years management experience. Salary range: $42-45,000, plus performance bonus.

matched with:

PLANT PERSONNEL MANAGER, responsible for labor relations, EEO compliance, training and development for all aspects of manufacturing operations. Degree in labor/industrial relations or plant management; minimum 5 to 7 years experience. Salary range: $40-42,000.

TELEMARKETING MANAGER, responsible for design and direction of new telemarketing operation; recruiting, training and supervising staff, selecting target lists, developing phone scripts. Minimum 5 years experience in telemarketing; management experience preferred but not essential. Salary range: $30-32,000.

matched with:

COMPUTER PROGRAMMER, to aid in developing special applications mainframe software and training staff in use thereof; degree in computer sciences or related field; entry level; hands-on mainframe experience required. Salary range: $26-28,000.

In Section II of this report we shall look at the data for each position individually, and examine how regional variations affect recruiting budgets. Our present purpose is to make informative comparisons among these various positions, and to find how costs vary by organizational size and turnover rates. To do so, we must now move to the body of the AMA questionnaire, the identical set of questions posed for each of these position descriptions.

Just as there were twelve position descriptions, the questionnaire sought data in twelve areas of inquiry. [This is coincidence; the writers see no ka'abalistic significance in the number twelve.] The questionnaire follows.

HIRING COSTS AND STRATEGIES: THE AMA REPORT

THE AMA HIRING COSTS AND STRATEGIES QUESTIONNAIRE

1. Please check <u>any</u> and <u>all</u> of the approaches you would use to fill this position in your organization:

    [ ]   A private employment agency, at a probable fee of $ _____ per $1,000 of salary.

    [ ]   An executive search firm, at a probable fee of _____ per cent of the first year's salary.

    [ ]   A public/community employment bureau, at a cost (if any) of $ _____ .

    [ ]   An in-house referral system, with a referral award (if any) of $ _____ .

    [ ]   An on-site or off-site open house, at an approximate cost of $ _____ .

    [ ]   A college recruitment program: [ ] which your organization has in place.
    　　　　　　　　　　　　　　　　　　　　[ ] which you would use at a fee of $ _____ .

    [ ]   Files of previous job applicants.

    [ ]   Posted listing to attract in-house applicants.

    [ ]   Other recruitment systems or techniques, and their approximate cost:
    _____ $ _____

2. How will you advertise for this position, and at what approximate cost? Check all you might use.

    [ ]   Local newspapers & magazines $ _____
    [ ]   Regional newspapers & magazines $ _____
    [ ]   National newspapers & magazines $ _____
    [ ]   Trade and professional journals $ _____
    [ ]   Other: _____ $ _____

3a. The recruiter assigned to fill this open assignment would earn
    an annual salary of $ _____

3b. How many open assignments would this recruiter carry concurrently?
    　　[ ] Less than 15   [ ] 15-25   [ ] 26-50   [ ] More than 50

4a. Travel, lodging and entertainment expenses for <u>candidates</u>
would total approximately: $_____

4b. Travel, lodging and entertainment expenses for <u>your recruiter</u>
would total approximately: $_____

5a. How many initial screening interviews would you expect to conduct
for this position? _____

5b. How many call-back (second) interviews would you expect to conduct? _____

5c. How many applicants would you expect to refer to the position
supervisor for further interviewing? _____

6. What form of testing, if any, would a candidate for this position receive?

    [ ] Job skill testing   [ ] Polygraph testing   [ ] Other: _____

    [ ] Psychological testing   [ ] Behavioral simulation testing   [ ] None

Your budget for testing for this position: $_____

7. Would you pay relocation expenses to fill this position?

    [ ] No   [ ] Yes $_____ (maximum)

8. What other direct costs might you encounter in filling this position?

_____ $_____

_____ $_____

_____ $_____

9. Which of these costs would be charged back to the department offering the position?

    [ ] Advertising   [ ] Recruiter Interview time

    [ ] Executive Search or Agency fees   [ ] Testing

    [ ] Candidates' Travel, Lodging and Entertainment   [ ] Relocation

    [ ] Recruiter Travel, Lodging and Entertainment   [ ] Other: _____

10. You would expect this position to be filled in approximately _____ weeks.

11. How would you rate your prospects of adequately filling this position with your first selection?

    [ ] Excellent: 90%-100% likelihood   [ ] Fair: 50%-75% likelihood

    [ ] Good: 75%-90% likelihood   [ ] Poor: Less than 50% likelihood

12. You would expect the person hired for this position to be "up to speed" in approximately:

    [ ] 1 month   [ ] 2-3 months   [ ] 4-6 months   [ ] 6 months-one year   [ ] More than one year

    The questionnaires were sent to evenly divided lists of <u>Personnel</u> Magazine subscribers in July 1985. Exactly 450 usable responses were received by August 15, our arbitrary cut-off date; 216 were Form A questionnaires, 234 were Form B. These 450 respondents gave us data for 1198 position choices, forming the database for this report.

HIRING COSTS AND STRATEGIES: THE AMA REPORT

1. Recruiting Strategies: The Favored Few

The first section of the questionnaire asked respondents to select the strategies they would use to fill the listed position -- exclusive of advertising, which was dealt with separately in Question 2. The questionnaire provided these choices:

- o   A private employment agency
- o   An executive search firm
- o   A public/community employment bureau
- o   An in-house referral system
- o   An on-site or off-site open house
- o   A college recruitment program
- o   Files of previous job applicants.
- o   Posted listing to attract in-house applicants.
- o   Other recruitment systems or techniques

Obviously, few recruiters would choose all or even half of these options to fill a given position. Most, in fact, choose three or fewer, in tandem with advertising; for all positions, the average was 2.82. Table 1 below shows the number of different approaches our respondents would choose to fill any position, and breaks the figures out in various respondent categories.

Number of Approaches Used In Recruiting
(All Positions)

Number of Recruiting Approaches	Total Sample	Annual Sales			Turnover Rate	
		+$500M	$50M to $500M	-$50M	+15%	-5%
One	20.4%	18.2%	15.1%	24.9%	24.8%	19.4%
Two	25.1%	26.2%	26.9%	23.1%	31.2%	23.0%
Three	25.5%	21.3%	27.7%	25.8%	21.7%	25.9%
Four	17.2%	21.8%	16.7%	15.5%	10.8%	18.4%
Five	7.0%	7.6%	8.5%	6.0%	8.2%	8.3%
Six	3.3%	3.1%	4.4%	2.7%	3.8%	.6%
Seven or more	1.6%	1.7%	.9%	2.0%	1.4%	2.5%

Table 1

HIRING COSTS AND STRATEGIES: THE AMA REPORT

Larger companies show an ever-so-slight tendency toward a greater number of options. The average number of approaches used to fill all positions by large companies -- that is, companies with more than $500 million in annual sales -- was 2.91, while small companies -- those with less than $50 million in annual sales -- averaged 2.72 different options. Economic activity made no difference (a 2.85 average for manufacturing companies, 2.82 for non-manufacturing firms).

Turnover rates, however, proved an important variable. Low turnover companies -- those reporting an annual turnover rate below five per cent -- followed significantly fewer recruitment paths than organizations with turnover rates above 15 per cent. This was especially true for the lesser-salaried positions: low-turnover companies averaged 2.1 different approaches for a staff accountant, while high-turnover firms averaged 3.1.

Generally, one respondent in five used a single approach; nearly half used one or two. The "full court press" was rare indeed: only one in a hundred respondents checked seven or more of the nine choices offered, and one company -- a mid-sized service organization -- checked all nine (which included "other"). This harried respondent has a high turnover rate, and is evidently ready to try anything more than once.

Interestingly, **the number of choices goes up as the salary comes down.** To fill the general manager's position at $80,000, respondents selected an average of 2.6 different approaches; for the Financial Officer at $60-65,000, the average was the same. But to fill positions at half the salary, the numbers were significantly higher: an average of 2.9 different approaches for the entry-level staff accountant, 3.0 for the $26-28,000 human resources specialist, and 3.1 for a computer programmer at the same salary. The highest average was for the $30-32,000 telemarketing manager -- 3.2 -- but for this position other factors were in play. The telemarketing job is the newest and least traditional of all those listed; little wonder that no national consensus has yet formed as to how to fill it.

Most recruiters, then, follow two or three options. Which do they choose? Certainly it depends upon the specific position to be filled. Few human resources managers would engage an executive search firm to look for an entry-level employee, and one does not ordinarily look for a senior financial officer through a college recruitment program. Yet the composite numbers for all positions are informative. When a position must be filled, six in ten of our respondents hit the files first, checking the credentials of previous job applicants; nearly half seek to fill the position from within. A third employ outside firms to aid in the search, and one in five looks to a government or community employment bureau for applicants. The combined numbers for all positions follow.

HIRING COSTS AND STRATEGIES: THE AMA REPORT

Preferred Approaches Used In Recruiting
(All Positions)

	Total Sample	Annual Sales +$500M	$50M to $500M	-$50M	Turnover Rate +15%	-5%
Files of previous job applicants	61.6%	61.8%	65.1%	58.6%	62.3%	51.0%
Posted listing for in-house applicants	47.0%	43.6%	52.1%	45.2%	49.4%	43.3%
An in-house referral system	41.2%	46.7%	41.8%	39.4%	46.8%	31.2%
A private employment agency	39.5%	43.1%	42.8%	36.7%	38.3%	42.0%
An executive search firm	31.0%	33.8%	34.9%	26.0%	30.9%	30.6%
A public/community employment bureau	21.9%	18.7%	17.7%	27.6%	23.2%	22.3%
A college recruitment program	17.3%	16.9%	16.2%	17.7%	17.8%	17.8%
An on-site or off-site open house	4.3%	5.3%	5.9%	2.7%	5.3%	2.5%
Other recruitment systems/techniques:						
Associations/conventions/job fairs	7.1%	7.1%	7.7%	7.2%	6.2%	8.9%
EEO or minority group agencies	0.9%	4.4%	.8%	.4%	.7%	.6%
Any other internal search	4.3%	7.6%	3.6%	2.3%	4.1%	1.3%
Networking/personal contacts	6.2%	2.2%	4.9%	8.3%	5.8%	9.6%

Table 2

Now, a closer look at each of these options, in order of preference.

Files of previous job applicants. By far the most favored of recruiting techniques after advertising, it is not without cost -- especially if the files are computerized, and regularly checked and updated. The payoff for such maintenance can be well worth the price. A major New York City utility operates under a demanding policy: every job vacancy **must** be filled within **two weeks**. It would not be possible without a regularly updated computer file of previous job applicants; with such a base, no position is long vacant.

The lesser numbers are for the higher-paying positions; no surprise there. There is, though, an extraordinary community of policy: for every position from entry to the $50,000 level, 60 to 70 per cent of our respondents hit the files first. The wild card in the numbers above concerns the telemarketing manager, a variant we shall see again and again for this newest of positions. Large company respondents see little purpose in checking the files here, for the position's requirements differ importantly from those for previous marketing posts.

HIRING COSTS AND STRATEGIES: THE AMA REPORT

Pct. of Respondents Who Would Check Files of Previous Job Applicants

	Total Sample	Annual Sales			Turnover Rate	
		+$500M	$50M to $500M	-$50M	+15%	-5%
All Positions	61.6%	61.8%	65.1%	58.6%	62.3%	51.0%
General Manager, $+80K	46.8%	33.3%	55.6%	42.4%	44.4%	45.5%
Senior Financial Off., $60-$65K	52.0%	47.1%	52.4%	53.6%	47.3%	42.9%
MIS Director, $55-60K	55.0%	59.3%	54.0%	54.9%	53.6%	53.3%
Purchasing Director, $47-$50K	64.6%	57.1%	65.0%	68.4%	72.7%	28.6%
Sales Manager, $42-45K	64.2%	63.6%	63.6%	64.3%	55.0%	58.3%
Plant Personnel Manager, $40-$42K	63.9%	59.3%	66.7%	64.3%	65.5%	40.0%
Product Manager, $35-$38K	64.8%	71.4%	75.9%	55.6%	62.5%	56.3%
Market Research Manager, $32-35K	69.6%	84.6%	72.4%	62.5%	75.7%	57.1%
Telemarketing Manager, $30-32K	63.6%	40.0%	71.4%	62.5%	66.7%	100.0%
Computer Programmer, $26-28K	70.1%	74.3%	71.2%	67.1%	74.7%	56.5%
Human Resources Specialist, $26-$28K	67.5%	66.7%	70.7%	62.2%	66.7%	85.7%
Staff Accountant, $24-26K	60.6%	75.0%	73.3%	49.0%	67.3%	27.3%

Table 3

This approach rates highest for every job save general manager, where it is second to using an executive search firm. That position, too, is the only one where fewer than half our respondents say they would check the files for candidates.

Posted listing for in-house applicants. The frequent promise to "promote from within" is a sometime thing. Just over half our respondents would post these positions to attract in-house candidates, and (as might be expected) the highest numbers are for the lower-salaried positions.

Fifty-seven per cent of our respondents look in-house for a staff accountant; only a third look there for a senior financial officer. The spread is as wide in large companies as in small ones. The figures confirm the conventional wisdom: the next step up is always more difficult than the last one. Companies are inclined to reach outside the organization to fill the jobs at the top.

HIRING COSTS AND STRATEGIES: THE AMA REPORT

Pct. of Respondents Who Would Post Listings for In-House Applicants

	Total Sample	Annual Sales			Turnover Rate	
		+$500M	$50M to $500M	-$50M	+15%	-5%
All Positions	47.0%	43.6%	52.1%	45.2%	49.4%	43.3%
General Manager, $+80K	27.4%	11.1%	50.0%	18.2%	37.0%	9.1%
Senior Financial Off., $60-$65K	33.3%	35.3%	35.7%	30.4%	37.8%	23.8%
MIS Director, $55-60K	54.2%	55.6%	56.0%	54.9%	47.8%	66.7%
Purchasing Director, $47-$50K	37.5%	14.3%	25.0%	57.9%	40.9%	57.1%
Sales Manager, $42-45K	37.0%	27.3%	27.3%	45.2%	52.5%	58.3%
Plant Personnel Manager, $40-$42K	45.4%	37.0%	50.0%	45.2%	49.1%	33.3%
Product Manager, $35-$38K	48.9%	35.7%	65.5%	42.2%	52.5%	31.3%
Market Research Manager, $32-35K	53.6%	61.5%	51.7%	50.0%	51.4%	57.1%
Telemarketing Manager, $30-32K	45.5%	40.0%	71.4%	37.5%	60.0%	0.0%
Computer Programmer, $26-28K	52.0%	48.6%	52.5%	53.9%	54.2%	60.9%
Human Resources Specialist, $26-$28K	57.3%	48.1%	65.9%	55.6%	56.1%	57.1%
Staff Accountant, $24-26K	57.4%	58.3%	66.7%	49.0%	61.5%	36.4%

Table 4

An in-house referral system. Our survey received two levels of response in this category. Four out of ten of our respondents maintain an in-house referral system; of those, half make cash awards part of the system. The amount varies, of course, position by position and company by company, but a consensus did emerge.

Naturally, the highest awards went for the highest-level position, that of general manager. The average there was $1,200, but some companies went significantly higher -- as high as $5,000. Far more typical were $500 awards for such posts as sales manager, market research manager, plant personnel manager . . . The average cash award for all positions was $370, but the modes -- the most frequently reported amounts -- frequently topped that figure by a goodly margin. What brought the averages down were comparatively small cash awards -- less than $250 -- for help in finding computer programmers, staff accountants, and human resources specialists, the entry-level jobs our survey encompassed.

HIRING COSTS AND STRATEGIES: THE AMA REPORT

As the chart below reveals, the highest report of in-house referrals has to do with filling the telemarketing post; for that position, cash awards come into play in three-quarters of the companies we surveyed. Once more this spot proves hard to fill, and companies seem willing to go to unusual lengths to find the right person for the job.

Pct. of Respondents Who Would Use an In-House Referral System

	Total Sample	Annual Sales			Turnover Rate	
		+$500M	$50M to $500M	-$50M	+15%	-5%
All Positions	41.2%	46.7%	41.8%	39.4%	46.8%	31.2%
General Manager, $+80K	41.9%	55.6%	27.8%	42.4%	44.4%	27.3%
Senior Financial Off., $60-$65K	40.7%	41.2%	35.7%	44.9%	45.9%	33.3%
MIS Director, $55-60K	32.8%	44.4%	34.0%	25.5%	36.2%	26.7%
Purchasing Director, $47-$50K	39.6%	71.4%	30.0%	36.8%	45.5%	28.6%
Sales Manager, $42-45K	54.3%	72.7%	63.6%	50.0%	65.0%	16.7%
Plant Personnel Manager, $40-$42K	33.3%	40.7%	30.6%	33.3%	38.2%	40.0%
Product Manager, $35-$38K	43.2%	50.0%	51.7%	35.6%	50.0%	18.8%
Market Research Manager, $32-35K	36.2%	53.8%	34.5%	29.2%	35.1%	51.1%
Telemarketing Manager, $30-32K	54.5%	80.0%	71.4%	37.5%	60.0%	100.0%
Computer Programmer, $26-28K	48.6%	40.0%	50.8%	51.3%	51.8%	39.1%
Human Resources Specialist, $26-$28K	41.0%	44.4%	43.9%	40.0%	49.1%	42.9%
Staff Accountant, $24-26K	40.4%	41.7%	46.7%	34.7%	48.1%	18.2%

Table 5

Use of a Private Employment Agency/Use of an Executive Search Firm. The two are so intricately connected that we cannot consider the one without the other. At the outset, a recruiter must choose whether or not to seek outside assistance; if the answer is yes, the very next choice concerns what kind of assistance to seek. It is generally but by no means universally true that an executive search firm is used to recruit senior managers, and employment agencies (public as well as private -- more of that to come) for middle managers, supervisors, and non-exempt employees. Yet one in three of our respondents would seek agency help in finding a senior financial officer (often in tandem with a search firm), and nearly as many -- 31.7 per cent -- would use an agency to recruit an $80,0000-a-year general manager. Moreover, a small but significant number of respondents would use search firms exclusively to fill the survey's entry-level positions: 7.7 per cent for a staff accountant, 3.6 per cent for a computer programmer.

HIRING COSTS AND STRATEGIES: THE AMA REPORT

This is partly a matter of nomenclature; there are no strict definitions, nationally recognized, that divide the two services. It is also geographic; there are areas where one or the other such businesses are the only game in town. As we shall see, the executive search firm is a somewhat more expensive option, but the price differential is not the prime determinant in making the choice; the service provided is.

Private Employment Agency/Executive Search Firm Options
(All Respondents)

	Private Agency Only	Search Firm Only	Used Both	Used Neither
All Positions	25.2%	18.0%	12.9%	44.0%
General Manager, $+80K	10.0%	45.0%	21.7%	23.3%
Senior Financial Officer, $60-$65K	18.9%	35.1%	16.2%	29.7%
MIS Director, $55-60K	21.1%	24.2%	24.2%	30.5%
Purchasing Director, $47-$50K	27.7%	14.9%	19.1%	38.3%
Sales Manager, $42-45K	21.0%	25.9%	11.1%	42.0%
Plant Personnel Manager, $40-$42K	22.6%	14.2%	10.4%	52.8%
Product Manager, $35-$38K	27.6%	14.9%	12.6%	44.8%
Market Research Manager, $32-35K	31.3%	10.9%	6.3%	51.6%
Telemarketing Manager, $30-32K	20.0%	25.0%	20.0%	35.0%
Computer Programmer, $26-28K	39.1%	3.6%	6.5%	50.9%
Human Resources Specialist, $26-$28K	22.1%	7.1%	7.1%	63.7%
Staff Accountant, $24-26K	30.8%	7.7%	7.7%	53.8%

Table 6

For the top positions, respondents prefer executive search firms to employment agencies by a goodly margin: 4.5:1 for a general manager, nearly 2:1 for a senior financial officer. Thereafter the ratios change dramatically: about 1:1 for the high-salaried MIS director or sales manager, and then 3:2 in favor of the agency for the plant personnel manager. When the offered salary drops below $40,000, the numbers go heavily for the agency: 3:1 for a market research manager or human resources specialist, 4:1 for a staff accountant ... 10:1 for the entry-level staff accountant.

In general, large companies are more likely to pay for outside recruiting help than small ones, as the charts on the following page will show. The exceptions: **none** of our large company respondents would use an employment agency to recruit a general manager, while 40 per cent of small companies would; instead, nine out of ten large companies would depend on search firms to fill such a post.

HIRING COSTS AND STRATEGIES: THE AMA REPORT

Pct. of Respondents Who Would Use a Private Employment Agency

	Total Sample	Annual Sales +$500M	Annual Sales $50M to $500M	Annual Sales -$50M	Turnover Rate +15%	Turnover Rate -5%
All Positions	**39.5%**	**43.1%**	**42.8%**	**36.7%**	**38.3%**	**42.0%**
General Manager, $+80K	33.9%	0.0%	38.9%	42.4%	29.6%	18.2%
Senior Financial Officer, $60-$65K	36.0%	35.3%	42.9%	33.3%	28.4%	52.4%
MIS Director, $55-60K	45.0%	48.1%	50.0%	41.2%	46.4%	40.0%
Purchasing Director, $47-$50K	47.9%	57.1%	65.0%	26.3%	40.9%	71.4%
Sales Manager, $42-45K	32.1%	45.5%	22.7%	33.3%	30.0%	25.0%
Plant Personnel Manager, $40-$42K	34.3%	51.9%	36.1%	21.4%	34.5%	46.7%
Product Manager, $35-$38K	40.9%	50.0%	31.0%	44.4%	35.0%	43.8%
Market Research Manager, $32-35K	39.1%	38.5%	48.3%	33.3%	40.5%	28.6%
Telemarketing Manager, $30-32K	45.5%	80.0%	57.1%	25.0%	46.7%	0.0%
Computer Programmer, $26-28K	48.0%	54.3%	49.2%	43.4%	50.6%	43.5%
Human Resources Specialist, $26-$28K	31.6%	33.3%	34.1%	31.1%	31.6%	50.0%
Staff Accountant, $24-26K	40.4%	33.3%	43.3%	40.8%	38.5%	27.3%

Table 7

Pct. of Respondents Who Would Use an Executive Search Firm

	Total Sample	Annual Sales +$500M	Annual Sales $50M to $500M	Annual Sales -$50M	Turnover Rate +15%	Turnover Rate -5%
All Positions	**31.0%**	**43.1%**	**34.9%**	**26.0%**	**30.9%**	**30.6%**
General Manager, $+80K	66.1%	88.9%	72.2%	57.6%	66.7%	72.7%
Senior Financial Officer $60-$65K	51.3%	67.6%	50.0%	42.2%	55.4%	33.3%
MIS Director, $55-60K	49.6%	44.4%	72.0%	29.4%	56.5%	26.7%
Purchasing Director, $47-$50K	33.3%	28.6%	40.0%	31.6%	22.7%	71.4%
Sales Manager, $42-45K	37.0%	36.4%	27.3%	38.1%	35.0%	33.3%
Plant Personnel Manager, $40-$42K	25.9%	29.6%	25.0%	23.8%	23.6%	40.0%
Product Manager, $35-$38K	27.3%	35.7%	27.6%	24.4%	25.0%	31.3%
Market Research Manager, $32-35K	20.3%	15.4%	24.1%	20.8%	21.6%	14.3%
Telemarketing Manager, $30-32K	45.5%	60.0%	14.3%	50.0%	40.0%	0.0%
Computer Programmer, $26-28K	9.6%	8.6%	13.6%	5.3%	6.0%	8.7%
Human Resources Specialist, $26-$28K	14.5%	14.8%	14.6%	15.6%	15.8%	14.3%
Staff Accountant, $24-26K	14.9%	16.7%	26.7%	8.2%	11.5%	18.2%

Table 8

HIRING COSTS AND STRATEGIES: THE AMA REPORT

In price comparisons, the modes -- the figures most frequently reported -- are more significant than the averages. For instance, the **average** fee an executive search firm would receive for recruiting a general manager was 26.5 per cent of the first year's salary, but the **mode** was significantly higher; half of our respondents would expect to pay more than 30 per cent, and one in ten budgeted 40 per cent of the first year's salary -- $32,000 to fill the $80,000-per-annum position. For the few companies that would use a private employment agency to fill that post, the **average** fee was $200 per thousand of salary, but the **mode** was $250 per thousand -- and only 21 per cent would pay a fee of $300 per thousand. Save for the very lowest salary levels, search firm fees are generally five to ten per cent higher than employment agency fees.

Here are the averages and modes by position for either service:

Agency/Search Firm Fees Paid
(in percentage of first year's salary)

	Employment Agency		Exec. Search Firm	
	Average	Mode	Average	Mode
All Positions	17.7%	25%	23.5%	30%
General Manager, $+80K	20.0%	25%	26.5%	30%
Senior Financial Off., $60-$65K	15.9%	20%	27.8%	30%
MIS Director, $55-60K	20.4%	25%	26.4%	30%
Purchasing Director, $47-$50K	16.0%	20%	24.3%	30%
Sales Manager, $42-45K	15.4%	20%	24.3%	30%
Plant Personnel Manager, $40-$42K	15.5%	15%	27.9%	30%
Product Manager, $35-$38K	20.8%	25%	23.2%	25%
Market Research Manager, $32-35K	19.2%	20%	23.6%	30%
Telemarketing Manager, $30-32K	19.1%	25%	22.2%	25%
Computer Programmer, $26-28K	16.3%	20%	23.7%	25%
Human Resources Specialist, $26-$28K	19.4%	25%	19.5%	15%
Staff Accountant, $24-26K	18.7%	20%	19.8%	15%

Table 9

The figures in the far right column above are remarkably consistent. Recruiters expect that an executive search firm will cost 30 per cent of salary for any position above $40,000 year; they expect to pay an employment agency significantly less. That helps explains why they prefer a search firm's services only for the topmost positions -- and also why search firms tailor their services for that market.

HIRING COSTS AND STRATEGIES: THE AMA REPORT

Fees are fees; high-turnover companies pay no more for either services than low-turnover companies, and large, medium, and small organizations budget like amounts for like assignments.

Public/Community Employment Bureaus. As a resource in filling all but the most senior positions, these public agencies proved nearly as valuable as private employment bureaus. To find a $28,000-per-year human resources officer, recruiters were as likely to turn to a public agency as a private one. For all positions, smaller firms depend on public agencies to a greater extent than larger ones; the trend is especially pronounced in the lesser-salaried range of jobs.

Pct. of Respondents Who Would Use a Public Employment Bureau

	Total Sample	Annual Sales			Turnover Rate	
		+$500M	$50M to $500M	-$50M	+15%	-5%
All Positions	21.9%	18.7%	17.7%	27.6%	23.2%	22.3%
General Manager, $+80K	9.7%	11.1%	5.6%	12.1%	7.4%	18.2%
Senior Financial Off., $60-$65K	11.3%	11.8%	7.1%	13.0%	12.2%	14.3%
MIS Director, $55-60K	26.0%	18.5%	20.0%	37.3%	24.6%	20.0%
Purchasing Director, $47-$50K	18.8%	28.6%	10.0%	26.3%	27.3%	28.6%
Sales Manager, $42-45K	17.3%	18.2%	13.6%	21.4%	17.5%	25.0%
Plant Personnel Manager, $40-$42K	18.5%	18.5%	11.1%	23.8%	20.0%	20.0%
Product Manager, $35-$38K	25.0%	21.4%	24.1%	26.7%	22.5%	31.3%
Market Research Manager, $32-35K	18.8%	7.7%	13.8%	33.3%	21.6%	0.0%
Telemarketing Manager, $30-32K	22.7%	20.0%	28.6%	12.5%	20.0%	0.0%
Computer Programmer, $26-28K	26.0%	22.9%	20.3%	34.2%	30.1%	21.7%
Human Resources Specialist, $26-$28K	32.5%	25.9%	29.3%	40.0%	33.3%	28.6%
Staff Accountant, $24-26K	31.9%	25.0%	26.7%	36.7%	30.6%	45.5%

Table 10

The low cost of dealing with public agencies is certainly an important factor in their popularity. Only a third of our respondents would anticipate any cost at all, and in most cases the fees are nominal; only five per cent would expect to pay more than $500 to fill any position.

College Recruitment Program. An obvious choice for the entry-level positions, college recruitment has its uses for the higher-salaried positions as well. Executives in mid-career attending continuing education programs, doctoral candidates who hold full-time corporate jobs, technicians learning new specialties -- organizations who cast their nets on college campuses have come up with surprising and rewarding catches. Fully ten per cent of our large-company respondents would test these waters to find a general manager -- not a high number, but not a negligible one either.

Still, college programs are prime feeders for the entry-level jobs, and large companies are not alone in their use of on-campus recruiters; about a third of our small-company respondents look to schools for staff accountants, computer programmers, and personnel officers. The numbers on the chart below offer no surprises in regard to the types of positions generally filled through college recruiting.

Pct. of Respondents Who Would Use a College Recruitment Program

	Total Sample	Annual Sales			Turnover Rate	
		+$500M	$50M to $500M	-$50M	+15%	-5%
All Positions	17.3%	16.9%	16.2%	17.7%	17.8%	17.8%
General Manager, $+80K	6.5%	11.1%	5.6%	6.1%	7.4%	9.1%
Senior Financial Officer, $60-$65K	6.7%	5.9%	4.8%	7.2%	6.8%	9.5%
MIS Director, $55-60K	8.4%	3.7%	12.0%	7.8%	10.1%	0.0%
Purchasing Director, $47-$50K	10.4%	0.0%	5.0%	15.8%	9.1%	14.3%
Sales Manager, $42-45K	7.4%	9.1%	4.5%	9.5%	7.5%	8.3%
Plant Personnel Manager, $40-$42K	9.3%	0.0%	5.6%	14.3%	7.3%	20.0%
Product Manager, $35-$38K	11.4%	7.1%	17.2%	8.9%	12.5%	12.5%
Market Research Manager, $32-35K	15.9%	15.4%	13.8%	20.8%	5.4%	14.3%
Telemarketing Manager, $30-32K	18.2%	20.0%	28.6%	0.0%	13.3%	0.0%
Computer Programmer, $26-28K	34.5%	42.9%	32.2%	31.6%	37.3%	47.8%
Human Resources Specialist, $26-$28K	28.2%	22.2%	24.4%	35.6%	31.6%	21.4%
Staff Accountant, $24-26K	35.1%	58.3%	30.0%	30.6%	38.5%	27.3%

Table 11

Costs of college programs vary widely, and it is difficult -- especially in the absence of a chargeback policy -- to estimate the cost of a single hire found through a campus recruiter. Most organizations that maintain college recruitment programs consider them

HIRING COSTS AND STRATEGIES: THE AMA REPORT

ongoing overhead items in the human resources divisional budget and, as such, not direct costs in the hiring process. Where direct costs are figured, they typically work out to under $1,500 per hire. Forty per cent of our respondents reported a direct cost-per-hire below $500 for on-campus recruiting of a computer programmer, and finding a staff accountant on campus cost half our respondents less than $750 per hire.

Another factor comes into play. College recruitment programs are designed to do more than fill particular entry-level positions. They also have to do with career-pathing and special executive training, with getting the best people into the organization for the long run. To both the organization and the individual, these factors may be more important than the specific duties the new hires will perform in their first year or two on the job. Graduates are selling not only their present skills but also those they will develop; recruiters are investing in the future.

<u>On-site or off-site open houses</u>. These did not prove significant options in the typical recruiting process. A bare minimum of respondents reported any such activity in filling most positions -- but the exception is revealing. Forty per cent of large company respondents in search of a telemarketing manager would arrange an open house to bring candidates together. For this new-style post, where qualifications are not strictly defined, large companies find the open-house approach viable -- even at a cost frequently in excess of $2,000.

Pct. of Respondents Who Would Use an On-Site or Off-Site Open House

	Total Sample	Annual Sales			Turnover Rate	
		+$500M	$50M to $500M	-$50M	+15%	-5%
All Positions	4.3%	5.3%	5.9%	2.7%	5.3%	2.5%
General Manager, $+80K	4.8%	11.1%	0.0%	6.1%	3.7%	9.1%
Senior Financial Officer, $60-$65K	2.7%	2.9%	2.4%	1.4%	2.7%	0.0%
MIS Director, $55-60K	3.8%	0.0%	8.0%	2.0%	7.2%	0.0%
Purchasing Director, $47-$50K	0.0%	0.0%	0.0%	0.0%	0.0%	0.0%
Sales Manager, $42-45K	7.4%	9.1%	13.6%	4.8%	7.5%	8.3%
Plant Personnel Manager, $40-$42K	1.9%	0.0%	0.0%	2.4%	1.8%	0.0%
Product Manager, $35-$38K	6.8%	7.1%	13.8%	2.2%	5.0%	6.3%
Market Research Manager, $32-35K	4.3%	0.0%	3.4%	8.3%	5.4%	0.0%
Telemarketing Manager, $30-32K	9.1%	40.0%	0.0%	0.0%	13.3%	0.0%
Computer Programmer, $26-28K	5.6%	8.6%	8.5%	2.6%	9.6%	0.0%
Human Resources Specialist, $26-$28K	4.3%	3.7%	4.9%	4.4%	3.5%	7.1%
Staff Accountant, $24-26K	3.2%	8.3%	6.7%	0.0%	3.8%	0.0%

Table 12

HIRING COSTS AND STRATEGIES: THE AMA REPORT

Other Recruitment Systems or Techniques. An open-ended query on the AMA questionnaire, it drew written responses from 18.5 per cent of all respondents. Most frequently cited was personal networking (6.2%), more highly favored for the mid-range positions than entry-level spots. Internal systems, a category combining automated searches, job data banks, and contacts with other corporate divisions or parent companies, found favor with 4.3 per cent of our respondents. Professional and trade associations shared a 3.6 per cent response with conventions and job fairs. Last on the list, mentioned by just one per cent of our sample, were contacts with EEO or minority group organizations. The figure may be tempered by noting that "public/community employment bureaus" were among the printed options on the questionnaire, and as such drew a 21.9 per cent response; nonetheless, ten of our respondents wrote in this additional item.

Summary: That which costs least is favored most. A check of the files is the first and favored step in filling a position, and in-house postings are number two; neither are high-cost practices. An open house is a comparitively high-ticket item; fewer than one respondent in twenty would hold one to help fill **any** of the offered positions. Employment agencies, which normally cost somewhat less than executive search firms, are a more frequent choice than the higher-priced option. Cost-conciousness is an important part of the recruiting process -- a fact which human resources managers can view with a combination of pride and concern. Finding the best person at the lowest cost: the balance is a fine one.

HIRING COSTS AND STRATEGIES: THE AMA REPORT

2. Advertising Costs and Practices

The AMA survey confirmed that newspaper and magazine advertising are by far the most widely employed of recruiting strategies, and the favored place to spend the budgeted recruiting dollar. The primacy of advertising holds across geographic lines and without regard to corporate size or activity. Generally, more ad dollars are spent in pursuit of the high-salaried executive, but the rule is by no means hard and fast. Some respondents would spend more money advertising for a $35,000-per-year product manager than for an MIS director earning nearly twice that salary.

There are two choices to be made: which of the available media (local, regional, national, and trade and professional) would be best for advertising the job at hand, and how much ought to be spent in each. As in the choice of recruiting strategies, the full-court press is as rare as the narrow path: few respondents advertise nowhere, and few everywhere. The typical choice for all but the lowest-salaried jobs is to advertise in two of the available media: locally, and in one of the three other vehicles, depending on the job to be filled. For the positions paying less than $30,000, the local option alone suffices for half our respondents.

Media Choices in Advertising Open Positions
(All Respondents)

	Local		Regional		National		Trade/Prof.	
	Pct.	Ave. Amt.	Pct.	Ave. Amt.	Pct.	Ave. Amt.	Pct.	Ave. Amt.
All Positions	85%	$900	44%	$1300	27%	$1700	36%	$1000
General Manager, $+80K	66%	1600	36%	1750	52%	1900	50%	1600
Senior Financial Off., $60-$65K	78%	1150	44%	1400	46%	2100	42%	1300
MIS Director, $55-60K	83%	950	48%	1400	41%	1750	53%	1100
Purchasing Director, $47-$50K	82%	900	52%	1350	36%	2000	41%	700
Sales Manager $42-45K	73%	1350	59%	1450	40%	1850	44%	1050
Plant Personnel Mgr., $40-$42K	82%	650	52%	1100	28%	1650	34%	1000
Product Manager, $35-$38K	83%	1000	50%	1700	18%	1300	39%	950
Market Research Manager, $32-35K	87%	800	47%	1100	31%	1100	45%	850
Telemarketing Manager, $30-32K	96%	1450	46%	1400	9%	xxx	41%	950
Computer Programmer, $26-28K	93%	800	34%	950	8%	1550	23%	1000
Human Resources Spec., $26-$28K	92%	700	40%	1000	14%	1150	25%	500
Staff Accountant, $24-26K	98%	700	21%	800	5%	300	12%	100

Table 13
(Dollar figures rounded to nearest $50)

HIRING COSTS AND STRATEGIES: THE AMA REPORT

All firms advertise. They do not, however, spend their dollars identically. Small companies put a greater share of their advertising budgets into local newspapers -- four out of five advertise locally for any post -- but only one in five would budget more than $1,000 for local space. Large firms are less likely to spend locally -- only half of them would -- but if they did, they'd spend twice as much on average.

The big firms depend on national advertising. Three-quarters of them would advertise for a senior financial officer in the national press and would budget an average of $2,500 to do it; less than a third of our small company respondents would go national, and most would spend no more than $1,000 on space. Mid-sized organizations are indeed in the middle: half would buy national advertising for the post. They'd spend with the large firms, though, typically budgeting $2,500.

Given this huge difference in the use of national advertising, it is surprising to note the similarities of choice in trade and professional journals as advertising media. For all positions, 36 per cent would allocate ad dollars to such journals; 38 per cent of mid-sized companies would do so, and 33 per cent of small firms. Again, the difference is in the dollar amounts. Large companies allocate an average of $1,750 for trade journal classifieds; mid-sized companies budget $1,000 on the average, and small companies $750. For the specific position of senior financial officer, the large companies would spend freely in trade journals, budgeting an average of $3,000, while both mid-sized and small company respondents would average just $800 for such space. Bear in mind, though, in this connection, that large companies are more likely to place large ads for multiple positions than their smaller competitors.

High turnover and low turnover companies make similar decisions on when to advertise, but the former allocate far more dollars to the task. For all positions, 87 per cent of the high turnover group would advertise locally, 82 per cent of low-turnover firms; but those with the higher rates would spend an average of $970 for local ad space, while those with a more stable workforce would average just $630. The contrast holds for regional ad space as well: $1,420 for the high turnover group, $1,150 for the low.

A company's location affects both advertising strategies and dollars expended. In the less populated areas of the West, recruiters sensibly spend more on national advertising than do their metropolitan brethren on either coast. Four out of ten survey respondents from Mountain States would allocate national advertising dollars for any of the twelve positions outlined in the survey; the average elsewhere is 28 per cent. Fully half the Rocky Mountain respondents would advertise in trade and professional journals; the figures shrink to 37 per cent of West Coast firms, 33 per cent in the North Atlantic region, and only 26 per cent of New England-based respondents.

The greater expense of national and trade advertising is offset somewhat by the lower costs of local advertising in the region. Mountain State respondents typically spent less than $250 in local ads; in the Midwest the average local budget was between $500 and

HIRING COSTS AND STRATEGIES: THE AMA REPORT

$750, and in New England the figure leaped to over $1,000. Indeed, nearly one in three New England respondents would spend over $2,000 on local ad space; none of the survey's Mountain State respondents would spend more than $1,000 locally.

What would be the shape of the typical advertising budget for a senior financial officer earning $65,000 a year? The most committed respondents would spend between $500 and $750 for local classified advertising, a like amount for regional ad space, and an additional two to three thousand dollars on both national and trade and professional press. The probable cost: $6,250.

But the survey sample offers wide variations. Ten per cent would do no advertising at all for the post, trusting to other recruiting techniques. Fewer than half would go beyond the local press if they were to advertise at all. The "typical" budget offered above represents the **mode**, the most frequent response; the **average** expense, once again, is significantly less. Table 13 above shows the average expenditures of **those who choose to advertise**; if we include in our figures those who would spend **no** ad dollars at all, the averages work out to $650 in local advertising, $540 regionally, $720 nationally and $345 in trade and professional journals: a total of $2,255. And this figure applies only to those who would advertise in all four areas; most respondents would choose only two -- local papers, and one other option.

To restate the obvious: the cost of advertising generally reflects the salary and responsibilities of the job to be filled. The average ad budget among all respondents to fill the plant personnel manager's post ($40-42,000 per annum) was $1,210; to find an entry-level computer programmer the average was $950. Again, these averages include respondents who would spend no advertising dollars at all in their search for candidates.

Clearly, the decision to advertise, and the allocation of advertising dollars, has a huge impact on the overall cost of hiring. A closer look at the figures for the post of plant personnel manager cited above gives ample proof. Just under 60 per cent of our respondents would advertise locally for that position; the decision to do so would cost an average of $635. Only a third of our sample would advertise for the job regionally; they'd spend an average of $1,110 to do it. Only 18 per cent of our respondents would advertise in national media or trade journals; once committed, they'd spend an average of $1,655 in the national press, and $975 in professional journals. Thus, depending on the degree of exposure the advertiser sought, the average cost of ad space could go as high as $4,375 -- and the sample turned up respondents willing to spend twice as much to find the plant personnel manager they desired.

Of all the recruiting strategies the survey studied, none were so variable as advertising practices, and none showed anywhere near the same range in costs. Advertising is very much a mixed bag, and the calculations made by individual human resources managers affect the cost-per-hire as no other single decision.

HIRING COSTS AND STRATEGIES: THE AMA REPORT

3. Recruiter Salaries and Work Loads

A variation on the classic formula for cost-per-hire may be performed with the data on the tables below, combined with data from Question 10 (the number of weeks in which the position ought to be filled). Begin with the recruiter's annual salary from Table 14; use it to obtain the weekly salary. Divide that by the number of concurrent cases carried (Table 15), and multiply the result by the number of weeks actually required to fill the job. The result, theoretically, yields the **labor** cost of the hire -- the only way to obtain the figure, unless the recruiter meters every moment on a given assignment. We perform the actual arithmetic in Section II of this report.

The data here contains few surprises. Assignments for the higher salaried positions go to senior human resources personnel, who also carry a somewhat lesser case load. Generally, the larger companies pay the higher salaries, and while there are variations in each particular position, on average high-turnover and low-turnover firms pay their recruiters about the same.

Annual Salary of Recruiter Assigned to Fill Open Position
(In Thousands of Dollars)

	Total Sample	Annual Sales			Turnover Rate	
		+$500M	$50M to $500M	-$50M	+15%	-5%
All Positions	$33.6	$37.2	$33.1	$32.0	$33.8	$33.3
General Manager, $+80K	$38.4	$38.0	$35.7	$39.7	$40.2	$33.4
Senior Financial Officer, $60-$65K	$37.7	$41.9	$39.2	$33.4	$38.9	$38.1
MIS Director, $55-60K	$34.3	$38.7	$33.2	$33.0	$36.1	$31.8
Purchasing Director, $47-$50K	$33.7	$43.2	$35.8	$29.4	$35.2	$31.8
Sales Manager, $42-45K	$35.8	$36.4	$38.7	$32.4	$37.8	$38.0
Plant Personnel Manager, $40-$42K	$34.3	$38.1	$35.8	$30.3	$32.6	$37.4
Product Manager, $35-$38K	$33.2	$37.8	$29.4	$34.7	$32.4	$29.8
Market Research Manager, $32-35K	$31.5	$34.6	$31.9	$28.9	$31.8	$29.9
Telemarketing Manager, $30-32K	$28.7	$33.8	$29.8	$24.6	$27.3	$30.0
Computer Programmer, $26-28K	$31.5	$34.5	$29.9	$30.5	$30.9	$32.5
Human Resources Specialist, $26-$28K	$31.3	$33.4	$29.5	$32.5	$31.5	$29.7
Staff Accountant, $24-26K	$31.4	$36.6	$31.4	$29.6	$30.2	$29.9

Table 14

HIRING COSTS AND STRATEGIES: THE AMA REPORT

Number of Open Assignments Recruiter Would Carry Concurrently

	Total Sample	Annual Sales			Turnover Rate	
		+$500M	$50M to $500M	-$50M	+15%	-5%
All Positions	15	19	15	13	15	13
General Manager, $+80K	14	11	16	14	14	12
Senior Financial Officer, $60-$65K	13	16	13	12	14	13
MIS Director, $55-60K	16	20	15	14	16	17
Purchasing Director, $47-$50K	15	23	15	12	15	10
Sales Manager, $42-45K	16	27	17	12	15	16
Plant Personnel Manager, $40-$42K	14	15	14	13	15	10
Product Manager, $35-$38K	15	25	16	12	16	15
Market Research Manager, $32-35K	16	17	17	13	17	15
Telemarketing Manager, $30-32K	13	16	12	11	12	10
Computer Programmer, $26-28K	16	21	17	13	16	13
Human Resources Specialist, $26-$28K	15	18	15	13	16	15
Staff Accountant, $24-26K	15	19	16	13	15	10

Table 15

It is worth noting in Table 15 that recruiters for the large companies carry a significantly higher case load than their mid-sized or small-firm brethren. Certainly the simple fact that large companies hire more people than do smaller ones in part accounts for the variation, which in some instances shows large-company recruiters handling **twice** the number of cases as small-company recruiters. In only one category is this trend reversed, that for the highest level position, the $80,000-per-year general manager. It is a finding that tends to confirm, rather than contradict, the rest of the chart: recruiting a major player becomes the responsibility of a senior human resources manager for whom recruitment is not a daily assignment.

Large companies pay higher recruiter salaries; large companies lay a larger assignment load on those recruiters. Paired together, the facts tend to equalize the labor cost-per-hire. Actually, they more than equalize the cost. The average salary the large company pays its recruiters for all positions given in the survey is 12 per cent higher than mid-sized company salaries and 18 per cent higher than what small companies pay, but the large company recruiter case load is **27** per cent above the mid-sized firm average, and 46 per cent greater than the average for small firms. What the large firms lose on the apples, they gain on the oranges.

4. Travel, Lodging and Entertainment

As the paired tables on the following pages will show, companies are far more willing to spend money on travel, lodging and entertainment for candidates than to send their own human resources personnel on the road. They are as eager to foot the bill for prospective sales and market research managers as for candidates for the very top spots, though the amounts budgeted for the lesser-paying jobs are correspondingly lower.

Allocations for candidates. Paying for lunch at very least, and for air fare and hotel accommodations where appropriate, is standard operating procedure for most respondents. More than half allocate such monies for all listed positions paying over $30,000. At the top of the list, a surprise: the sales manager's job. Seventy-three per cent of our respondents would budget T&E for those candidates, comfortably above the 65 per cent that would pay expenses for a prospective general manager.

The dollar amounts tell a different story. For the GM post the average candidate T&E budget is $2,425, for the sales job, $1,525; for the senior financial officer, $1,750, for the MIS director, $1,525. The correlation between the rank of the offered post and the **willingness** to budget for candidate travel, lodging and expenses is not strict; the correlation between the rank and the **amount** budgeted is far more exact.

Allocations for recruiters. On the average only one company in four budgets travel, lodging and entertainment expenses for recruiters, and the amounts are less than half of those allocated for candidates. Again, it's the sales manager who rates most highly: 42 per cent of our respondents would pay a recruiter's expenses in this job search, against 35 per cent who would pay recruiter T&E to find a general manager.

This special attention to the sales manager's spot in both expense categories invites analysis. Is it because sales personnel spend the greater share of the corporate T&E budget that the human resources department, in turn, spends a disproportionate amount of the recruiter budget on taking salesmen to lunch? It is an unscientific but attractive hypothesis: perhaps recruiters want to see a salesman's act, performed in its natural setting.

Summary. These are significant amounts of money, in some cases rivaling advertising budgets. Example: combined candidate-recruiter T&E for filling the purchasing director's post averages $1,525, whereas the average combined cost of local and trade advertising for the same spot is $1,600. At the high end, combined T&E for the prospective general manager totals $3,700 -- a considerable sum. Easily overlooked, travel and entertainment is an important expense item in the recruitment process.

Budget Allocations for Candidate Travel, Lodging and Expenses

	Total Sample		Over $500M		Annual Sales $500M - $50M		Below $50M		Turnover Rate Above 15%		Below 5%	
	Pct.	Ave. Amt.	Pct.	Ave. Amt.	Pct.	Ave. Amt.	Pct.	Ave. Amt.	Pct.	Ave. Amt.	Pct.	Ave. Amt.
All Positions	59.5%	$1,225	69.4%	$1,725	64.7%	$1,200	52.7%	$1,025	64.4%	$1,200	49.1%	$1,000
General Manager, $+80K	65.1%	$2,425	77.8%	$4,425	67.7%	$2,400	58.8%	$1,975	70.4%	$2,100	58.3%	$2,375
Senior Financial Off., $60-$65K	69.3%	$1,750	87.9%	$2,200	65.9%	$1,450	64.9%	$1,725	71.1%	$1,725	44.1%	$1,225
MIS Director, $55-60K	69.1%	$1,525	62.9%	$1,625	82.0%	$1,725	61.5%	$1,275	75.4%	$1,525	60.0%	$1,075
Purchasing Director, $47-$50K	66.7%	$1,125	57.1%	$1,075	78.9%	$1,650	60.0%	$ 550	63.6%	$1,150	42.9%	$1,100
Sales Manager, $42-45K	72.8%	$1,525	91.7%	$1,900	69.6%	$1,425	70.2%	$1,475	78.0%	$1,600	57.1%	$1,075
Plant Personnel Mgr., $40-$42K	51.8%	$1,325	76.9%	$2,125	64.1%	$1,200	45.7%	$ 850	63.6%	$1,300	47.1%	$ 750
Product Manager, $35-$38K	62.0%	$1,425	64.3%	$2,700	66.7%	$1,500	48.9%	$ 975	64.3%	$1,425	44.4%	$1,175
Market Research Mgr., $32-35K	65.3%	$1,050	68.8%	$1,300	74.2%	$1,325	55.6%	$ 550	69.0%	$ 950	71.4%	$ 660
Telemarketing Manager, $30-32K	58.2%	$ 950	80.0%	$1,125	28.5%	$ 500	70.0%	$1,150	73.3%	$1,300	33.3%	$ 250
Computer Programmer, $26-28K	44.4%	$ 650	47.1%	$1,325	53.3%	$ 575	38.3%	$ 400	47.6%	$ 725	28.0%	$ 450
H.R. Specialist, $26-$28K	45.0%	$ 800	55.6%	$1,050	48.8%	$ 750	36.9%	$ 600	57.6%	$ 750	64.3%	$1,000
Staff Accountant, $24-26K	36.4%	$ 300	50.0%	$ 350	46.7%	$ 325	29.4%	$ 275	37.7%	$ 300	25.0%	$ 75

Columns marked Pct. show the percentage of respondents who make budget provisions for candidate T, L & E; columns marked Ave. Amt. show the average amount those respondents would spend.

Table 16

Budget Allocations for Recruiter Travel, Lodging and Expenses

| | Total Sample | | Annual Sales | | | | | | Turnover Rate | | | |
| | | | Over $500M | | $500M - $50M | | Below $50M | | Above 15% | | Below 5% | |
	Pct.	Ave. Amt.	Pct.	Ave. Amt.	Pct.	Ave. Amt.	Pct.	Ave. Amt.	Pct.	Ave. Amt.	Pct.	Ave. Amt.
All Positions	26.5%	$ 575	39.6%	$1,000	26.1%	$ 600	21.9%	$ 375	29.9%	$ 575	18.6%	$ 475
General Manager, $+80K	34.9%	$1,275	66.7%	$2,075	44.4%	$1,625	23.5%	$ 750	33.3%	$ 950	25.0%	$1,250
Senior Financial Off., $60-$65K	32.7%	$ 950	45.5%	$1,250	31.8%	$1,075	27.0%	$ 650	36.8%	$1,050	21.7%	$ 250
MIS Director, $55-60K	26.8%	$ 475	33.3%	$ 325	32.0%	$ 600	19.2%	$ 475	31.9%	$ 525	26.7%	$ 575
Purchasing Director $47-$50K	31.3%	$ 400	28.6%	$1,000	36.8%	$ 450	25.0%	$ 225	40.1%	$ 375	28.6%	$ 200
Sales Manager, $42-45K	42.0%	$1,075	58.3%	$2,050	43.5%	$1,600	40.4%	$ 625	43.9%	$1,175	28.6%	$1,150
Plant Personnel Mgr., $40-$42K	28.9%	$ 550	50.0%	$1,050	17.9%	$ 425	19.6%	$ 175	40.0%	$ 700	11.8%	$ 175
Product Manager, $35-$38K	20.5%	$ 550	28.6%	$1,175	23.3%	$ 650	18.4%	$ 275	26.2%	$ 500	11.1%	$ 275
Market Research Mgr., $32-35K	25.6%	$ 325	37.5%	$ 175	22.5%	$ 250	25.9%	$ 525	23.8%	$ 150	42.9%	$1,075
Telemarketing Manager, $30-32K	33.3%	$ 500	40.0%	$1,200	14.3%	$ 200	30.0%	$ 300	40.0%	$ 700	33.3%	$ 250
Computer Programmer, $26-28K	18.4%	$ 400	32.4%	$1,250	18.3%	$ 250	14.8%	$ 150	23.8%	$ 500	8.0%	$ 150
H.R. Specialist, $26-$28K	18.3%	$ 450	25.9%	$ 750	13.9%	$ 350	19.6%	$ 375	16.9%	$ 275	28.6%	$ 550
Staff Accountant, $24-26K	12.5%	$ 100	33.0%	$ 225	16.7%	$ 100	5.9%	$ 50	11.3%	$ 75	0.0%	$ 0

Columns marked Pct. show the percentage of respondents who make budget provisions for recruiter T, L & E; columns marked Ave. Amt. show the average amount those respondents would spend.

Table 17

5. Screening Interviews and Referrals

There is a remarkable unanimity in the matter of the number of initial screening interviews the recruiters would conduct for each position, and the number that would be referred to the position supervisor for further consideration. The table below, which records averages rounded to the nearest unit, has a very narrow range. In every case in the total sample, between eight and ten candidates would be interviewed, and three or four would go on to meet the position supervisor. The findings do not differ importantly by company size or by turnover rate. In terms of the open position, the search for a general manager commands the greatest number of initial interviews; second is that elusive commodity, the telemarketing manager.

Number of Initial Screening Interviews -- Number Referred to Position Supervisor

	Total Sample	Annual Sales			Turnover Rate	
		+$500M	$50M to $500M	-$50M	+15%	-5%
All Positions	8 - 4	8 - 4	9 - 4	8 - 4	9 - 4	8 - 3
General Manager - $+80K	10 - 3	11 - 4	11 - 3	9 - 4	9 - 4	12 - 3
Senior Financial Officer - $60-$65K	8 - 4	9 - 4	7 - 4	8 - 4	9 - 3	7 - 3
MIS Director - $55-60K	8 - 4	7 - 4	9 - 4	7 - 4	7 - 4	7 - 4
Purchasing Director - $47-$50K	9 - 4	9 - 4	9 - 4	8 - 4	9 - 3	10 - 4
Sales Manager - $42-45K	9 - 4	10 - 4	9 - 4	8 - 4	10 - 4	8 - 3
Plant Personnel Manager - $40-$42K	8 - 3	7 - 3	9 - 3	8 - 4	8 - 3	8 - 3
Product Manager - $35-$38K	8 - 4	9 - 4	9 - 4	7 - 4	8 - 3	8 - 4
Market Research Manager - $32-35K	9 - 3	9 - 4	9 - 3	8 - 4	9 - 4	8 - 3
Telemarketing Manager - $30-32K	10 - 3	11 - 2	13 - 4	7 - 3	10 - 3	6 - 4
Computer Programmer - $26-28K	8 - 4	9 - 4	8 - 4	8 - 3	9 - 3	8 - 3
Human Resource Specialist - $26-$28K	9 - 4	9 - 5	10 - 3	8 - 4	8 - 4	12 - 4
Staff Accountant - $24-26K	8 - 4	8 - 4	9 - 4	7 - 4	8 - 4	9 - 4

Table 18

When the numbers are so alike, the analyst wonders why. What is it about these numbers -- eight to ten screening interviews, three or four referrals onward -- that cuts across all the variables? Is there another way of looking at the figures that will yield a different result? When the means, or averages, pose a problem, the modes, or most frequent answers, often suggest a solution. To the first question -- "How many initial screening interviews would you expect to conduct for this position?" -- the mode response was ten, given by 20.3 per cent of the whole sample; the second most frequent response was five, given by 12.1 per cent. People do tend to answer such questions in multiples of five; with this in mind, we can safely say that the actual range across our sample is wider than the narrow "eight to ten" the averages show; that, in fact, ten screening interviews is on the high side of the survey, eight more typical, and five by no means unusual.

Using the same approach for the second part of the question -- "How many applicants would you expect to refer to the position supervisor for further interviewing?" -- the mode response was three, given by 37.9 per cent of our respondents; next was not four, as the average would suggest, but **two**, cited by 22.3 per cent of the sample, followed by five (14.0%) and then, finally, four, given by just 10.9 per cent of our respondents.

The conclusion: while the averages show a narrow range, the modal responses reveal that in actual practice recruiters are more likely to refer just two candidates to position supervisors, from a screening pool that is frequently as low as five applicants, and rarely higher than ten.

Nevertheless, modal analysis confirms that the numbers do not change significantly by open position, organization size, or turnover rate. The survey results still show a remarkable similarity of practice in this area of the recruitment process.

6. Testing in the Recruitment Process

CLOSE-UP ON TESTING: ITS FUTURE IN THE WORKPLACE

by John Aberth
Editorial Associate

Most survey respondents do no testing at all. Of those who do test, the majority will only make a small financial investment ($400 average) in their programs (see Figure 1).

Human resource managers agree that the Equal Employment Opportunity Commission (EEOC) is responsible for this reluctance to test. Says Michael Schreweis, manager of human resources at Robinson Nugent, Inc., a mid-size electronics manufacturer in New Albany, Indiana, "They're afraid the EEOC is going to rake them over the coals, and if they misuse the tests, they probably would get raked over the coals. There's nothing in Title 7 [of the EEOC Act] that says you can't test, but if you do test and use the results in your decision, you damn well better have the validation to back it up." Apparently, most companies don't want to spend the time or the money for this validation.

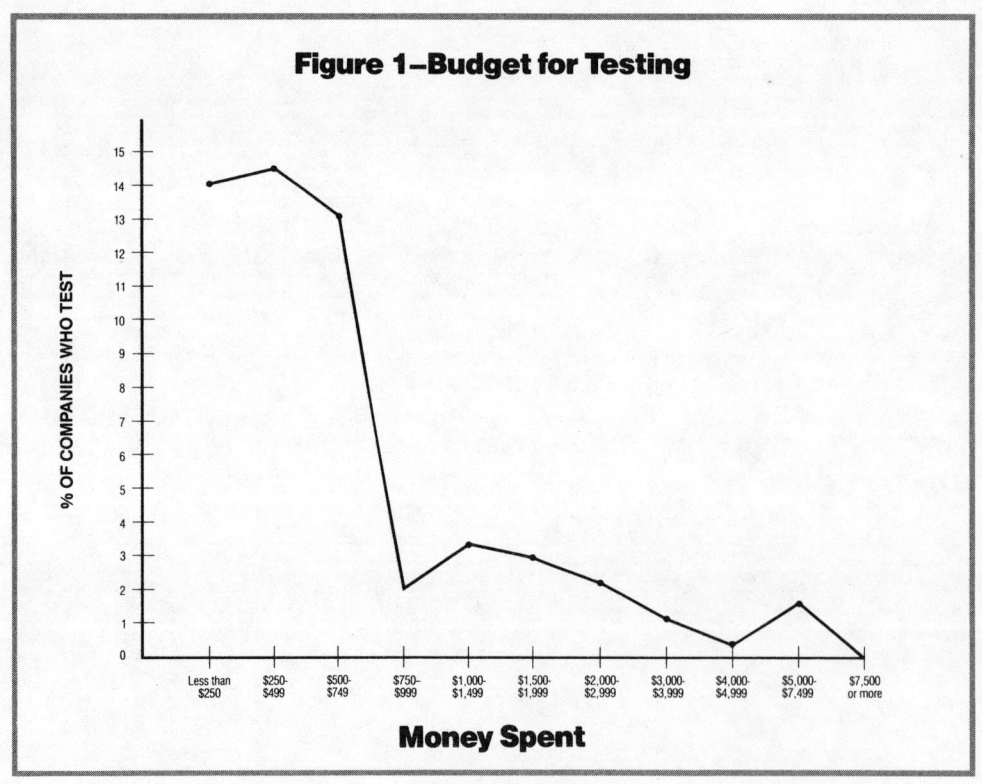

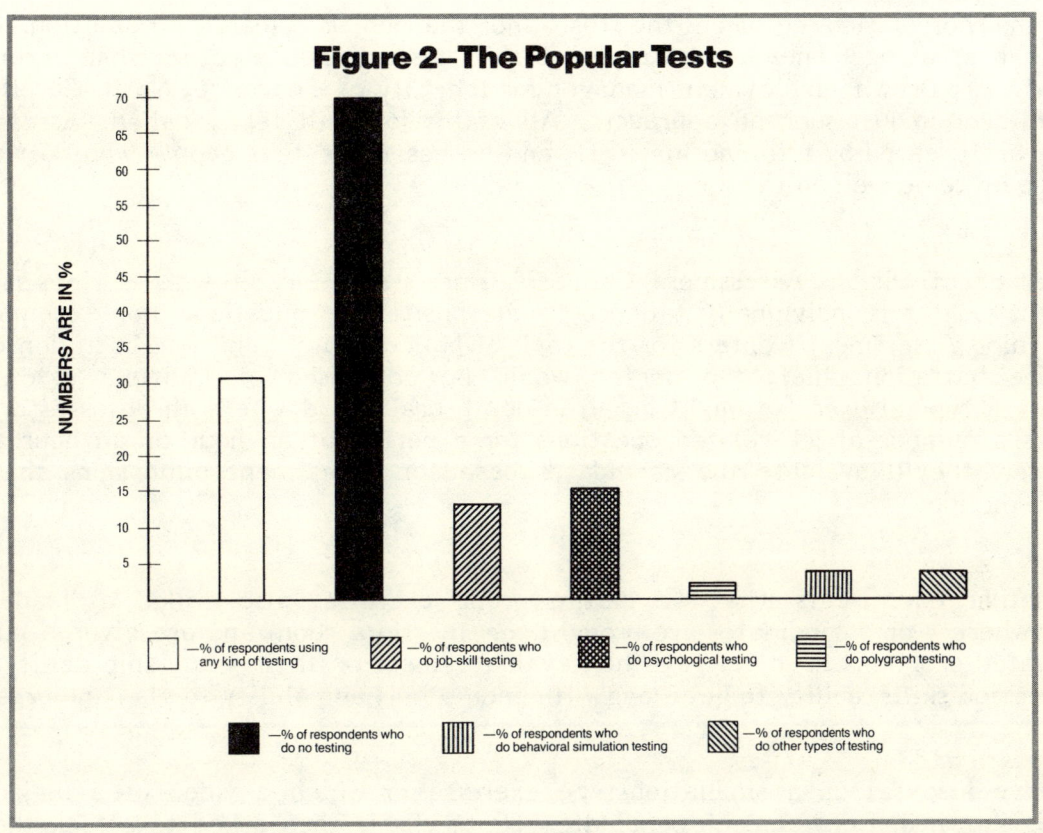

Some companies, like Kidney Care, Inc., a small health care organization in Jackson, Missouri, do testing on a very informal basis -- orally rather than written. Art Pullum, personnel director at Kidney Care, describes his testing this way: "Basically, we'll talk with the candidates, talk the jargon and see how the person would react in a given situation." Thus, job-skill or psychological questions are made part of the interviewing process, and the direct cost of testing procedures is eliminated. Mr. Pullum believes that most of the companies that have dropped testing still do it on this informal basis.

Ralph Thompson, personnel manager for Detex Corporation, a small industrial manufacturing company in New Braunfels, Texas, offers another solution. His company does testing, but only <u>after</u> the candidate has been hired, when he is an employee. Says Thompson, "Our aim is to see how fitted the person is to the position he or she is already in." Any question of validation is academic, since the testing is not part of the actual hiring process. Still, Thompson believes the test results are accurate and useful, helping him to gain an insight into the employee.

The Popular Tests

A quick glance at Figure 2 and one can see that psychological and job-skill tests comprise almost all of the testing still in existence. Their popularity can be easily explained. Job-skill testing, which usually involves confronting applicants with some aspect of the job and then observing how they react, is easily validated with the EEOC because the correlation between the test and the job is clear. In addition, many companies are saving money by creating job-skill tests in-house rather than through a consultant. Art Brown, employment manager for the City of Charlotte, North Carolina, is a firm believer in just such an approach. All of his job-skill tests, called "Assessment Centers," are created by him and his staff, and he has found that people who do well on the test go on to do well on the job.

What exactly is an "Assessment Center?" Here's how Mr. Brown describes it: "An Assessment Center is individually tailored to the position in question. For example, we try to develop Assessment Centers for the rank of police captain and fire battalion chief. For a fire battalion chief, the center would be composed of multiple assessment exercises. A typical exercise might be an in-depth oral board where three assessors ask candidates a number of job-related questions for a period of an hour or an hour and a half. Later, they'll evaluate the candidates based on assessment dimensions that are related to the job.

"Another exercise is what we call a group exercise, also called a 'leaderless' exercise, where 4 or 5 candidates are brought together in a room and are given a number of job-related problems to solve. We then evaluate them on their leadership ability, oral communication skills, ability to get along with each other, and ability to plan and organize.

"We've also set up a simulation-type exercise in which a video of a major fire disaster is shown in front of each candidate. He or she is then asked to attack the fire using certain resources such as ladder trucks, fire engines, and supply lines. This way we can observe and evaluate them on how they react under pressure."

The popularity of the psychological test is harder to understand, however. The content of such a test can vary widely, from asking how a candidate would handle a given situation (similar to job-skill) to assessing the candidate's personality through such questions as "Which would you rather do, go to a party or go to a business meeting?" June Gibson, personnel manager at North, Inc., a small health care company in Philadelphia, Pennsylvania, says the aim of their psychological tests is to get the mental "healthiness" of the people they hire, to make sure they can "function in a professional type atmosphere."

Undoubtedly, the subjective nature of these tests makes them hard to validate. There is an indication that many companies are becoming dissatisfied with their psychological tests and are planning to phase them out. The E.J. Brooks Company, another small industrial manufacturing organization, located in Newark, New Jersey, stopped its psychological testing just this year. Barbara Tomeo, Brooks' personnel director, explains why: "The test was administered by an outside service and consisted of two parts: one part measured motivational drive and the other measured conscientiousness. We had problems with the motivational part. The positions being tested were in our sales division, and we found that the people which the test told us would be gung ho actually didn't have the personality for salesmanship. In fact, we kept only two out of the ten people we hired through the test.

"I would say that this experience has turned us totally off psychological testing. From now on, the only tests we're going to use are the form tests, the ones that measure vocabulary, spelling, etc. Other than that, we'll do personal interviews, which I think is the only reliable way to assess an individual's personality." Ms. Tomeo also mentioned that the difficulty of validating psychological tests was another contributing factor in her company's decision.

A February, 1985 article in one of the leading magazines for personnel management called the use of polygraph testing in the workplace "significant." The results of our survey, however, point to a different conclusion. Of those respondents who test, only 1.7 per cent do polygraph testing, the lowest percentage on the chart. According to the Personnel Magazine article, 26 states currently have laws restricting the use of the polygraph, and more are expected to enact such laws. In addition, public opinion is generally against polygraph use. These two factors perhaps explain our low figure. However, the polygraph-users we talked to believe their companies will continue to use polygraph testing as long as the state legislatures allow them to do so.

Behavioral simulation likewise has a low percentage of use among the businesses who do testing. Some personnel professionals consider behavioral simulation just another name for job-skill testing; if true, our survey results must be read in that light. However, Dr. Edward A. Powers, faculty member of AMA's Institute for Management Competency, says there is a difference between the two: "The job-skill test is more of a respondent test -- very quantitative and measurable -- that is generally given to mechanical or technical people. Behavioral simulation, on the other hand, tends to be an operant exercise that measures a diverse range of skills. One of the goals of behavioral simulation is to recreate the environment in which the candidate will be working. An example is AT&T's 'in-basket' exercise, in which candidates are given 10 memos in the in-basket and they then have to prioritize the memos according to their perceived importance. Of course, there is no absolute 'right' answer to these exercises."

Michael Schreweis agrees that there is a distinction to be made: "Our job-skill tests are generally for the lower level jobs, the production and hourly people. The behavioral simulation test is more for our managerial and professional positions. With behavioral simulation, we're trying to see how individuals react to real-life situations -- situations that have actually happened at our company and in which we know what works and what doesn't work. Even if people don't come up with the right answers, the basic reasoning or logic they used to get there is what's important. Actually, we've had candidates come up with better solutions than the ones we already had, and thus we've been able to learn from them." However, he agreed that human resource people often treat the two as one and the same.

Testing by Position

How is the testing distributed among the different position descriptions offered in the survey? The most dramatic result we found is that computer programmers receive an enormous amount of job-skill testing -- 20 per cent more than the average for all the positions. Computer programmers are relatively easy positions to test: you just ask the candidate to run a program. In general, the lower level positions, such as staff accountant, human resource specialist, and computer programmer, received the highest percentage of job-skill testing in our survey.

On the other hand, psychological testing is especially popular with the higher level positions: financial officer, purchasing director, sales manager, and general manager. General manager had the highest percentage of testing, about 10 percent above the average. The follow-up interviews we conducted support our conclusion: Companies are more likely to give job-skill testing for the entry-level type positions; for the seasoned positions, they will assume that the candidate already has the job skills and thus will try to probe deeper with the more esoteric psychological test. "We certainly don't put our managers through the performance testing we give for entry-level clerical jobs," says Alan Orr, personnel director for the Santa Clara County office of education. Michael Schreweis points out that "the skill test is more equipped for those on the lower level, while the psychological test is more applicable to the management positions. I think a lot of companies are looking for the one test, the one paper and pencil test that they can give to everybody."

Our survey showed that financial officers and sales managers receive the most polygraph testing. Behavioral simulation testing is prevalent in the plant personnel manager and telemarketing manager positions.

Testing by Category of Organization

In our sample, diversified conglomerates and the government/military bureaus are the biggest users of job-skill testing (see Figure 3). Art Brown of the City of Charlotte agrees that government agencies like to test; however, he complains that "the testing is probably more limited than most government agencies would like due to lack of resources and funding." One would expect a city's police and fire departments to require testing, particularly job-skill, because their positions are high-risk and require the employees to work under pressure. Therefore, the departments would want to ensure that they have hired proven, competent candidates.

Psychological testing is popular in the consumer manufacturing and the trade divisions. Earlier we found that sales managers are among those who receive a high degree of psychological testing. Thus, it would seem that industries that rely on selling for their bread and butter use psychological testing to discover candidates with the "salesman's personality."

Banking is by far the biggest user of the polygraph, accounting for over a third of all polygraph use. Robert Lloyd, senior vice-president of First American National Bank in Kingsport, Tennessee, explains why his company uses the polygraph: "What we are doing when we subject candidates to the polygraph is basically setting the stage, putting a mindset in their heads. Then if there's a cash shortage later on, everyone that was involved in the transaction or had access to the safe knows that he or she is going to take the polygraph again."

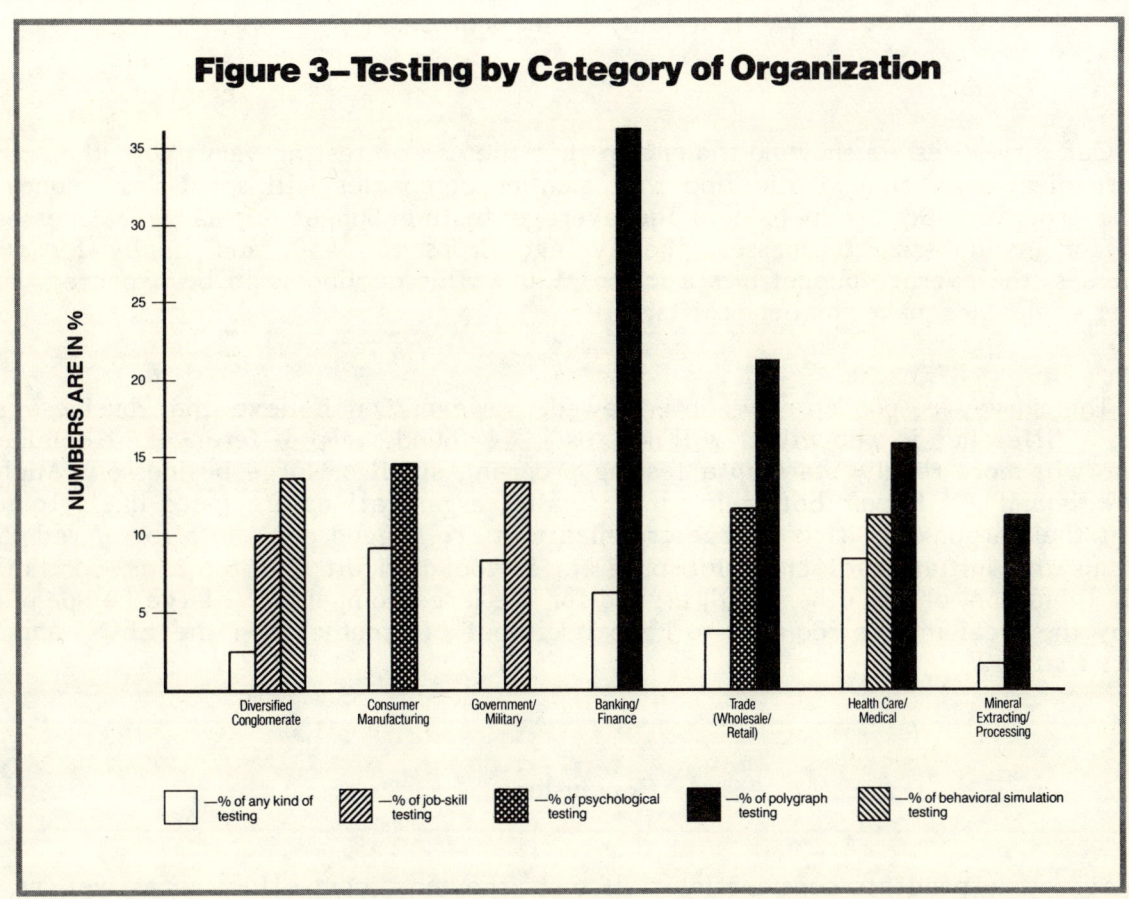

Figure 3—Testing by Category of Organization

Mr. Lloyd goes on to assess the usefulness of polygraph testing: "I think the polygraph is effective as one of a series of tests. But I don't think our hiring or terminating decision in a case of question should be based on the polygraph. It's not dependable enough. If you have an investigation and essentially you catch somebody with their hand in the till, they can still go back and pass the polygraph test. We've had this happen at the bank. So if all the results of the investigation are positive with the exception of the polygraph, I think you have to act on the preponderance of evidence. I don't think the polygraph should make or break your decision."

The wholesale/retail, the mineral extracting, and the health care/medical industries are also big users of the polygraph. In the wholesale/retail industry, polygraph testing is to be expected since the companies are hiring people who will be handling money, such as cashiers and sales personnel.

Marshall Jones, director of human resources at the Merry Health Center in Oklahoma City, Oklahoma, had mixed reactions to our health care/medical statistic: "My knowledge is that other hospitals and health care providers use the polygraph in a remedial sense, when they suspect somebody of diverting drugs illegally. I know a lot of places use it for that. But I would be surprised if they used it for employment purposes."

In the behavioral simulation category, our survey found that diversified conglomerates, education, and health care/medical companies were by far the biggest users.

HIRING COSTS AND STRATEGIES: THE AMA REPORT

Testing by Business Size

Our survey results show no indication that the use of testing varys with the size of the organization. Still, we did find that smaller companies will spend less money on testing programs already in place. The average testing budget for large businesses is $900; for medium-size businesses, the average drops to $450; and finally for small businesses, the average budget hits a low of $200. This decline is to be expected, since smaller companies make smaller profits.

The survey respondents we interviewed, however, do believe that business size makes a difference in who will or will not test. We found sharp differences of opinion as to who will more readily start-up a testing program, small or large businesses. Michael Schreweis and Art Pullum both think that smaller organizations are more likely to test. One of their arguments is that large organizations are bogged down in a lot of red tape, and thus the initiation of a testing program is too difficult and too time-consuming. Ralph Thompson, on the other hand, argued for the large company: "A large company can employ the legal muscle required to keep itself out of trouble with the EEOC and the powers that be."

Conclusion

Survey respondents consider job-skill tests the most cost-effective as well as the most reliable tests, but only for lower level positions. There is probably no reliable test for higher managers or CEOs. However, some human resource people have said that psychological tests do give their companies a certain comfort level with their choices, which may contribute to their success.

HIRING COSTS AND STRATEGIES: THE AMA REPORT

7. Relocation Expenses

Nowhere else did we find such wide variation among respondents as in this category. At the top end, more than a quarter of our respondents would set no maximum dollar amount for relocation expenses, and stated a willingness to spend "whatever it takes" to get the right person for the job. At the other extreme, 40 per cent would allocate no monies at all in this area.

Our question was stated in two parts: would the respondent pay relocation expenses for the position? If so, what would be the **maximum** figure allowed? In both instances the figures varied, naturally, with the position at issue. Over 80 per cent of respondents would shoulder such expenses for a new general manager, and over 60 per cent would do so for all the positions paying more than $35,000 a year.

When we asked for maximum figures we found that one respondent in four set no maximum. However, it cannot be said that companies are free and easy with expenditures in this column. Just under ten per cent of our respondents put a $5,000 cap on relocation expenses, and another 12 per cent reported caps between $5,000 and $15,000. For the general manager's position, just over half would go above the $25,000 mark in relocation costs.

Maximum Budgeted Amounts for Relocation Expenses
(All Respondents)

	$0	Below $5K	$5K - $15K	$15K - $25K	Above $25K	Set No Maximum	Mean* (000)
All Positions	40.2%	9.7%	12.1%	5.8%	6.0%	26.1%	$13.0
General Manager, $+80K	18.3%	5.0%	13.3%	10.0%	25.0%	28.3%	$23.2
Senior Financial Off. $60-$65K	23.0%	12.5%	14.5%	6.6%	13.2%	30.2%	$16.1
MIS Director, $55-60K	24.4%	11.0%	15.7%	8.7%	8.0%	32.2%	$13.5
Purchasing Director $47-$50K	22.9%	8.3%	16.7%	0.0%	2.0%	50.0%	$7.0
Sales Manager, $42-45K	20.0%	14.1%	18.8%	3.5%	5.9%	37.6%	$11.4
Plant Personnel Manager, $40-$42K	37.7%	7.9%	9.6%	7.9%	6.1%	30.7%	$15.1
Product Manager, $35-$38K	40.4%	7.9%	19.1%	4.5%	5.6%	22.5%	$11.9
Market Research Manager, $32-35K	37.0%	10.9%	10.9%	15.1%	4.1%	21.9%	$11.4
Telemarketing Manager, $30-32K	45.5%	22.7%	4.6%	0.0%	4.6%	31.8%	$4.2
Computer Programmer, $26-28K	64.8%	8.5%	6.8%	3.4%	1.2%	15.3%	$8.9
H. R. Specialist, $26-$28K	55.0%	9.9%	9.9%	5.4%	1.8%	18.0%	$8.2
Staff Accountant, $24-26K	75.0%	5.4%	5.4%	1.0%	0.0%	11.9%	$6.2

*Mean rounded to nearest $100

Table 19

HIRING COSTS AND STRATEGIES: THE AMA REPORT

The primary reason for the range of reponses in this category is the very wide variety of such expenses. There is more at issue here than travel to the new work area and reimbursement for professional movers. In some cases relocation expenses may include purchasing the candidate's old house or a new one in the new location, providing for dual residences for a period of time, prolonged hotel expenses or apartment rentals . . . it mounts up. Averages have diminished meaning when the responses are so varied.

As Table 20 below makes clear, large and mid-sized companies are competitive, while small ones trail in their willingness to spend at all in this category, and certainly to spend without a set limit.

The discretion of the human resources officer continues to be the single most important factor in the cost of hire. The impact of a decision in this area -- to spend or not to spend, and if so, how much -- can make a $100,000 difference. In no other category is the ante so high.

Respondents Who Budget Relocation Expense Funds / Respondents Who Set No Maximum

	Total Sample		+$500M		Annual Sales $50M to $500M		-$50M	
	Bdgt. Funds	No Max.	Bdgt. Funds	No Max.	Bdgt. Funds	No Max.	Bdgt. Funds	No Max.
All Positions	59.8%	26.1%	68.5%	30.6%	67.8%	31.5%	49.7%	18.6%
General Manager, $+80K	81.7%	28.3%	77.8%	33.3%	94.1%	47.1%	78.1%	21.9%
Senior Financial Officer, $60-$65K	77.0%	30.2%	88.2%	35.2%	85.7%	40.4%	66.2%	18.3%
MIS Director, $55-60K	75.6%	32.2%	73.1%	38.5%	87.8%	30.6%	63.3%	26.5%
Purchasing Director, $47-$50K	77.1%	50.0%	85.7%	57.1%	85.0%	60.0%	73.7%	42.1%
Sales Manager, $42-45K	80.0%	37.6%	75.0%	41.6%	91.7%	54.2%	72.7%	25.0%
Plant Personnel Manager, $40-$42K	62.3%	30.7%	77.8%	33.3%	76.9%	41.0%	42.2%	20.0%
Product Manager, $35-$38K	59.6%	22.5%	76.9%	19.2%	65.5%	31.0%	51.1%	14.9%
Market Research Manager, $32-35K	63.0%	21.9%	68.8%	25.0%	73.3%	20.0%	47.8%	17.4%
Telemarketing Manager, $30-32K	54.5%	31.8%	60.0%	40.0%	33.3%	16.7%	66.7%	22.2%
Computer Programmer, $26-28K	35.2%	15.3%	52.9%	17.6%	39.7%	22.4%	20.8%	7.8%
Human Resource Specialist, $26-$28K	45.0%	18.0%	47.8%	21.7%	47.5%	10.0%	42.2%	20.0%
Staff Accountant, $24-26K	25.0%	11.9%	41.7%	16.7%	31.0%	13.8%	16.7%	8.3%

Table 20

HIRING COSTS AND STRATEGIES: THE AMA REPORT

8. Other Direct Costs

Just one in ten of our respondents listed additional costs to those reported for Questions 1 through 7. As Table 21 on the following page demonstrates, large companies were far more likely to include such costs in their hiring budgets than were the less sizable organizations. Turnover rates, too, proved an important variable, with high-turnover organizations reporting nearly twice the costs, on average, of the low-turnover group.

House-related expenses, including temporary living costs, were most frequently listed. So far as they could be identified, these have been factored into the relocation expenses previously reported. The responses here are as much a matter of terminology as corporate policy; one company's "relocation" costs may be another's "miscellaneous"."

Slightly over 20 per cent of respondents listing "other" costs -- that is, just two per cent of the whole sample -- called them "miscellaneous." Smaller numbers still assigned costs to pre-employment screening, and one-half of one per cent of all respondents put bonus payments in this category.

The position-by-position averages on Table 21 must be viewed through the focus of this very low number of respondents. The samples are so small that these averages are not statistically valid as national benchmarks. It is certainly not true that the national average of large companies' "other" costs in hiring general managers is nearly $10,000, while their average "other" costs for hiring a purchasing director is zero. Nevertheless, the figures are informative as a picture of our respondent sample in itself (rather than as a miniature of a wider view). The figures exaggerate, but do not distort, the differences in "other" costs from position to position; it is certainly true here, as in other categories, that more monies are expended in hiring general managers than staff accountants.

And it is also true that the wild cards elsewhere play that part here. The sales manager's position continues to draw expenses out of proportion to the salary offered; this was the case for relocation expenses, for both candidate and recruiter travel, lodging and entertainment, and for advertising expenses. Although fifth on the salary scale of our offered positions, Section II will reveal that the hiring cost of a sales manager is comparative to that for a senior financial officer earning half again the salary, and as such is second only to the general manager's post.

-43-

Budget Allocations for Other Direct Costs

	Total Sample		Annual Sales						Turnover Rate			
			Over $500M		$500M - $50M		Below $50M		Above 15%		Below 5%	
	Pct.	Ave. Amt.	Pct.	Ave. Amt.	Pct.	Ave. Amt.	Pct.	Ave. Amt.	Pct.	Ave. Amt.	Pct.	Ave. Amt.
All Positions	8.7%	$1225	17.0%	$3550	21.8%	$ 575	27.5%	$ 975	20.4%	$1325	28.6%	$ 750
General Manager, $+80K	11.1%	$3550	11.1%	$9900	11.1%	$ --	8.8%	$1800	18.5%	$1425	0.0%	$ --
Senior Financial Off., $60-$65K	7.7%	$1950	5.8%	$5200	6.8%	$ 400	10.8%	$1550	7.9%	$2900	17.4%	$1325
MIS Director, $55-60K	12.1%	$ 800	11.1%	$ 675	8.0%	$ 650	15.3%	$1150	11.5%	$ 450	20.0%	$ 400
Purchasing Director $47-$50K	12.5%	$ 800	0.0%	$ --	15.7%	$ 750	15.0%	$ 850	9.1%	$1000	0.0%	$ --
Sales Manager, $42-45K	9.1%	$2500	8.3%	$7000	8.7%	$ 650	8.5%	$2300	9.8%	$3725	14.2%	$2500
Plant Personnel Mgr., $40-$42K	9.6%	$1150	7.4%	$5000	7.6%	$ 750	13.0%	$ 550	5.4%	$3000	29.4%	$ 375
Product Manager, $35-$38K	11.8%	$1500	7.4%	$4950	10.0%	$1050	12.2%	$ 475	9.5%	$ 775	16.6%	$ 200
Market Research Mgr., $32-35K	8.9%	$ 825	0.0%	$ --	6.4%	$ 200	14.8%	$ 975	9.5%	$ 150	0.0%	$ --
Telemarketing Manager, $30-32K	4.2%	$1000	0.0%	$ --	0.0%	$ --	0.0%	$1000	6.7%	$1000	0.0%	$ --
Computer Programmer, $26-28K	4.9%	$ 900	0.0%	$ --	3.3%	$ 150	7.4%	$ 475	5.9%	$1525	12.0%	$ 100
H.R. Specialist, $26-$28K	10.8%	$ 500	8.3%	$ 100	11.6%	$ 625	13.0%	$ 475	10.2%	$ 450	21.4%	$ 400
Staff Accountant, $24-26K	7.3%	$ 325	0.0%	$ --	6.6%	$ 100	7.8%	$ 500	5.6%	$ 225	0.0%	$ --

Columns marked Pct. show the percentage of respondents who make budget provisions for other recruiting expenses; columns marked Ave. Amt. show the average amount those respondents would spend.

Table 21

9. Chargeback Policies

There are no position-by-position comparisons to be made in this category. A policy is a policy; what is charged to the various departments for a high-salaried post is similarly charged for the lesser-paid positions. Nor is turnover a factor. Size ought to be; studies of other subjects have revealed that larger companies generally have more complex and exact chargeback policies than mid-sized or small ones. With a single exception, this proved not to be the case in accounting the hiring costs. Instead, we found a remarkable similarity across the board; large, mid-sized, and small organizations practice the same chargeback patterns.

Here is another confirmation of a central finding of this study: that although hiring **costs** generally vary according to organization size, hiring **strategies,** and the policies by which those strategies are pursued, are remarkably similar, regardless of size. This community of practice is uncommon; it indicates that at least where hiring is concerned, there is a near-universal discipline at work in the human resources function.

The exception is found in relocation costs. Nearly 60 per cent of large and mid-sized companies charge these expenses back to the department seeking the new hire; just over one-third of smaller companies do so.

Recruitment Costs Charged Back to Departments

	Total Sample	Annual Sales		
		+$500M	$50M to $500M	-$50M
Advertising Costs	68.4%	61.9%	67.5%	72.7%
Agency Fees	50.9%	51.2%	55.8%	47.6%
Candidate Travel, Lodging & Ent.	54.8%	55.4%	59.1%	52.4%
Recruiter Travel, Lodging & Ent.	17.1%	17.3%	20.1%	14.8%
Recruiter Interview Time	10.9%	7.1%	12.4%	10.5%
Relocation	47.1%	57.7%	58.0%	36.3%
Testing	8.0%	8.9%	10.2%	5.5%

Table 22

The obvious pattern revealed here is that monies expended directly on human resources personnel -- that is, recruiter travel, lodging and entertainment and recruiter interview time -- are absorbed into the human resources budget, whereas monies expended elsewhere (to the candidate, agencies, advertising media, etc.) are charged to the various departments. Testing costs are also usually paid by human resources.

HIRING COSTS AND STRATEGIES: THE AMA REPORT

10. Filling the Position: The Time Factor

The amount of time it takes to fill an open position has a direct effect on hiring costs in the **labor** cost -- that is, the amount of time the recruiter must spend on the various aspects of filling that post, expressed as a percentage of the recruiter's salary. There are other costs to the organization as a position goes unfilled, but these cannot be viewed as hiring costs. As stated earlier, the labor cost is factored into the position analyses in Section II of this report.

Asked their expectations, respondents reported an average eight-week span from the time the managerial opening is posted to the time it is filled. The uppermost span was ten weeks for the two highest slots, the general manager and the senior financial officer; the staff accountant average was five and a half weeks. There were no important differences in these expectations by organizational size or turnover rate, or by geographic location.

Number of Weeks To Fill Position
(All Respondents)

Weeks:	1-3	4-5	6-7	8-9	10-12	+12	Mean
All Positions	8.1%	23.5%	21.0%	17.5%	19.3%	10.7%	8.0
General Manager, $+80K	5.0%	10.0%	11.7%	21.7%	28.3%	21.2%	10.0
Senior Financial Off., $60-$65K	2.6%	10.3%	28.2%	16.0%	23.7%	19.2%	10.0
MIS Director, $55-60K	3.8%	13.6%	19.7%	12.1%	29.5%	6.8%	9.8
Purchasing Director, $47-$50K	6.1%	28.6%	24.7%	20.4%	12.2%	8.2%	7.3
Sales Manager, $42-45K	3.4%	23.0%	18.4%	18.4%	24.1%	12.6%	8.6
Plant Personnel Mgr., $40-$42K	3.5%	26.5%	22.1%	24.8%	12.4%	8.7%	7.7
Product Manager, $35-$38K	9.0%	28.1%	16.9%	15.7%	23.6%	7.2%	7.5
Market Research Manager, $32-35K	6.8%	20.3%	27.5%	16.2%	24.3%	6.8%	7.9
Telemarketing Manager, $30-32K	13.0%	21.7%	8.7%	8.7%	39.1%	2.8%	9.6
Computer Programmer, $26-28K	17.5%	31.6%	16.9%	19.8%	11.3%	23.3%	6.3
Human Resource Spec., $26-$28K	8.1%	27.9%	26.1%	16.2%	16.2%	5.2%	7.2
Staff Accountant, $24-26K	17.4%	38.0%	22.8%	15.2%	4.3%	2.2%	5.5

Table 23

HIRING COSTS AND STRATEGIES: THE AMA REPORT

11. Filling the Position: The First Selection Factor

The costs of hiring for a particular position are, of course, significantly affected if the first candidate selected for the post proves less than adequate. Most, if not all, of the hiring costs must be borne once more when the position again becomes vacant.

Respondents were less than optimistic about their prospects of getting the right person the first time out. As Table 24 on the following page displays, only a bit more than a third of them rated their chances of doing so as "excellent" (which the questionnaire defined as a 90 per cent chance of adequately filling the position with the first selection). Just over half rated the chances "good" (a 75% to 90% chance), and a tenth called their prospects only "fair" (no better than a 75% chance).

Although hiring at the top end of the scale would cost more time and more money -- and involve more highly paid recruiting talent, either in-house or through an agency -- respondents are not particularly more optimistic about senior managers than juniors. Just the opposite, in fact: the only spot for which half our respondents found the first-selection prospects "excellent" was the lowest salaried, the entry-level staff accountant. Next was the human resources specialist; the chances there were rated "excellent" by very nearly half the sample. Perhaps the human resources managers who filled out our questionnaire are most confident hiring within their own function. Of the rest, only the plant personnel manager, at $40 - $42,000 a year, scored over 40 per cent "excellent" in this category.

There were no important differences by organizational size, but there were vital ones between low-turnover and high-turnover companies. The most dramatic difference concerned the purchasing director's job: more than **twice** as many low-turnover companies (57.1%) thought their first selection had an "excellent" chance than the high-turnover sample (26.1%). The figures for the sales manager were nearly as different: 42.9 per cent of the low-turnover group checked "excellent" in this category, while 26.2 per cent of the high-turnover sample did so. For the other positions paying $40,000 or more, the margin differentiating the groups was generally ten per cent. Where the findings reversed at the lower end of the scale -- that is, for the market research manager and the staff accountant -- the samples are smallest and least reliable.

Experience is the best teacher. High-turnover companies expect to stay that way; they hire in hope but, apparently, hope in vain. It is not the hiring process that causes the high turnover. Other elements in the corporate environment are responsible for that. Yet it is surprising that our survey found little difference between these two groups -- high-turnover and low-turnover firms -- in either costs or strategies. They are going about things the same way, to different results. Perhaps they oughtn't.

Ratings of Prospects of Adequately Filling Position with First Selection

	All Respondents			+500M			Annual Sales $50M - $500M			Below $50M		
	Exc.	Good	Fair	Exc.	Good	Fair	Exc.	Good	Fair	Exc.	Good	Fair
All Positions	36.9%	53.6%	9.6%	37.3%	49.3%	13.3%	38.2%	52.0%	9.8%	36.0%	56.4%	7.6%
General Manager, $+80K	32.8%	60.7%	6.6%	22.2%	55.6%	22.2%	29.4%	70.6%	0.0%	33.3%	60.6%	6.1%
Senior Financial Off., $60-$65K	36.3%	50.3%	13.4%	29.4%	44.1%	26.5%	47.7%	43.2%	9.1%	33.8%	56.8%	9.5%
MIS Director, $55-60K	23.5%	64.4%	12.1%	40.7%	51.9%	7.4%	22.0%	64.0%	14.0%	17.3%	69.2%	13.5%
Purchasing Director, $47-$50K	36.7%	53.1%	10.2%	28.6%	42.9%	28.6%	30.0%	55.0%	15.0%	45.0%	55.0%	0.0%
Sales Manager, $42-45K	28.1%	64.0%	7.9%	16.7%	66.7%	16.7%	41.7%	50.0%	8.3%	25.5%	70.2%	4.3%
Plant Personnel Manager, $40-$42K	45.1%	46.9%	8.0%	38.5%	50.0%	11.5%	53.8%	35.9%	10.3%	42.2%	53.3%	4.4%
Product Manager, $35-$38K	35.2%	57.1%	7.7%	42.9%	50.0%	7.1%	33.3%	60.0%	6.7%	34.0%	57.4%	8.5%
Market Research Manager, $32-35K	31.1%	60.8%	8.1%	56.3%	37.5%	6.3%	21.4%	71.4%	7.1%	26.9%	61.5%	11.5%
Telemarketing Manager, $30-32K	30.4%	52.2%	17.4%	40.0%	40.0%	20.0%	57.1%	14.3%	28.6%	11.1%	77.8%	11.1%
Computer Programmer, $26-28K	35.9%	51.4%	12.7%	26.5%	64.7%	8.8%	36.7%	46.7%	16.7%	40.0%	50.0%	10.0%
Human Resource Spec., $26-$28K	47.4%	46.6%	6.0%	46.2%	42.3%	11.5%	41.5%	53.7%	4.9%	52.2%	43.5%	4.3%
Staff Accountant, $24-26K	53.7%	43.2%	3.2%	58.3%	33.3%	8.3%	53.3%	43.3%	3.3%	54.0%	44.0%	2.0%

Table 24

HIRING COSTS AND STRATEGIES: THE AMA REPORT

12. Up To Speed Expectations

The numbers we obtained here do not affect hiring costs, even indirectly. Yet they are part of the recruiter's thinking not just at the end of the hiring process, but throughout. They go to the very essence of the decision to hire a particular candidate, the last decision in the long process that began with the choices of strategies which we investigated at the beginning of this section. It can be fairly said that the hiring process is not complete until the newly hired person is up-to-speed, doing the job as required and expected. How long, then, until this can be said?

Less than four months, on average, for a computer programmer, say our respondents; more than six for a market research manager. The mode -- the most frequent response -- was four to six months, and the overall average 4.9; a significant number put it up to a year, while one in five companies hiring a computer programmer expect him or her to be up to speed in a month.

"Up To Speed" Expectations
(All Respondents)

Months:	1	2 - 3	4 - 6	6 - 12	+ 12	Mean
All Positions	7.2%	35.9%	33.3%	21.3%	2.4%	4.9
General Manager, $+80K	3.0%	27.3%	39.4%	24.2%	6.1%	5.8
Senior Financial Off., $60-$65K	0.0%	37.8%	35.1%	25.7%	1.4%	5.2
MIS Director, $55-60K	3.8%	25.0%	34.6%	32.7%	3.8%	5.9
Purchasing Director, $47-$50K	0.0%	30.0%	60.0%	10.0%	0.0%	4.7
Sales Manager, $42-45K	2.1%	38.3%	38.3%	21.3%	0.0%	4.8
Plant Personnel Mgr., $40-$42K	11.1%	33.3%	42.2%	13.3%	0.0%	4.3
Product Manager, $35-$38K	8.5%	36.2%	31.9%	19.1%	4.3%	4.9
Market Research Manager, $32-35K	3.8%	23.1%	30.8%	30.8%	11.5%	6.7
Telemarketing Manager, $30-32K	11.1%	33.3%	44.4%	11.1%	0.0%	4.2
Computer Programmer, $26-28K	20.0%	43.8%	23.8%	12.5%	0.0%	3.6
Human Resource Spec., $26-$28K	4.3%	43.5%	21.7%	23.9%	6.5%	5.3
Staff Accountant, $24-26K	12.0%	40.0%	28.0%	20.0%	0.0%	4.3

Table 25

SECTION II

HIRING COSTS: THE KEY INDICATORS

Section I of this report dealt with options and expenses -- the choices that human resources managers make in the hiring process and the costs that follow from those choices. In this section, the matter is all dollars. The amounts displayed in these charts are average anticipated expenditures by respondents **who would opt to spend money in these categories.** A true average would include respondents who spend nothing, but the figures would be less useful as national and regional guidelines. Human resources managers must make two choices in categories such as agency fees, referral awards, advertising, and the like: first, to spend or not to spend; then, how much to spend.

Labor Cost/Hire. As we report our findings, we produce a new figure for each position: the **labor cost of hire.** This figure is derived from three other numbers given by our respondents:

o   The **annual salary** of the recruiter assigned to fill the open position. This figure (presented in Chapter 4 of Section I) is divided to give a weekly salary, then furthur divided by:

o   The **concurrent case load** the recruiter carries while working to fill the open position (also from Chapter 4 of Section I). The result gives that part of the weekly salary earned in filling the open position. This is then multiplied by:

o   The expected **number of weeks** necessary to fill the position. The result is a theoretical Labor Cost/Hire, presented here in combination for all positions:

ALL POSITIONS	Total Sample	Annual Sales			Turnover Rate	
		+$500M	$50M to $500M	-$50M	+15%	-5%
Recruiter's Annual Salary	$33,580	$37,180	$33,060	$32,020	$33,830	$33,250
Concurrent Case Load	15.0	18.6	15.2	12.7	15.2	13.4
Weeks to Fill Position	7.9	8.5	8.4	7.5	8.3	8.3
Labor Cost/Hire	$340	$326	$351	$364	$355	$396

Table 26

HIRING COSTS AND STRATEGIES: THE AMA REPORT

The figure, of course, is inexact. It is built on the unrealistic assumption that a recruiter carrying a case load of 15 will spend exactly the same amount of time every week on each of the positions. We know that that is not true -- but at the same time it **is** true that a recruiter carrying a case load of 20 is **quantitatively** more productive than one carrying a case load of 12. And we see that large companies, while paying their recruiters markedly higher salaries, often produce a lower cost-per-hire than smaller firms because the recruiters carry a heavier case load. The same is true of organizations with a high turnover rate.

The Labor Cost/Hire, therefore, is useful as a comparative index. The pages that follow break out the LC/H by organization size and by turnover rate. In a few cases the differences are particularly marked: for instance, the LC/H for a general manager works out to $744 for a large company and $410 for a mid-sized firm, by far the largest differential we found. While the difference is huge in terms of percentage, in actual dollar outlay it is $334 -- not an outrageous figure in a process that allots fifty times that amount or more for executive search firm fees, and a hundred times more for relocation expenses. In most instances the spreads are far less extreme.

<u>National/Regional Figures.</u> Along with the nationwide averages, each positional chart lists the average expenditures in ten regions. These regions generally align with the first digit of the postal ZIP code. The exceptions are in the 0 column: Puerto Rico and the Virgin Islands are not included in those figures, and New Jersey respondents have been factored out of the 0 file and placed instead with New York and Pennsylvania in the 1 column. For the convenience of the reader, here are the the states represented by each ZIP code (an alphabetical list of states may be found at the end of this section):

0 (New England): Maine, New Hampshire, Vermont, Massachusetts, Rhode Island, Connecticut.

1 (North Atlantic): New York, New Jersey, Pennsylvania.

2 (Mid Atlantic): Maryland, Delaware, District of Columbia, Virginia, North Carolina, South Carolina

3 (South): Tennessee, Georgia, Florida, Alabama, Mississippi.

4 (Midwest): Ohio, Indiana, Michigan, Kentucky.

5 (North Central): Wisconsin, Minnesota, Iowa, North Dakota, South Dakota, Montana.

6 (Mid Central): Illinois, Missouri, Nebraska, Kansas.

HIRING COSTS AND STRATEGIES: THE AMA REPORT

7 (South Central): Louisiana, Arkansas, Oklahoma, Texas

8 (Rocky Mountain): New Mexico, Arizona, Colorado, Utah, Wyoming, Idaho, Nevada.

9 (Pacific): California, Oregon, Washington, Alaska, Hawaii.

Insufficient Samples. As a statistical sample narrows, so also does the utility of its averages. That rule should be borne in mind when reading the charts that follow. These charts parse things pretty fine -- the average testing budget for a product manager in the Rocky Mountain States, for instance -- and in some cases the sample simply loses any claim to validity. Such an average would misinform rather than enlighten, and where the sample is so very small these charts show a ++ rather than a number.

The appearance of a ++ is occasionally instructive. For example, in the chart for the general manager's post, half of our regions show no sample for employment agency fees, and more than half show none for in-house referral awards. These signs are quick reminders of the statistics developed in Section I -- that few respondents opt for an employment agency in filling this position, while conversely few use executive search firms to find an entry-level staff accountant.

Reading the Charts. No respondent would pay all the amounts in a column. Obviously, none would pay both an agency and a search firm -- it would be one or the other -- and, as we have seen, about half would use neither service and pay nothing at all in this area. Similarly, in advertising, few respondents would budget money in all four media; the typical choice is two, in various mixes of local, regional, national and trade/professional. The charts give averages in **each** of these categories, but adding up **all** the figures in a column would **not** give an average total expenditure.

Another word on advertising: the same newspaper may represent different things to different respondents. For example: to a Chicago-based service organization, the **Chicago Tribune** is a local newspaper; to a Milwaukee manufacturer, it's a regional vehicle; to an Atlanta consultancy , it's a national buy; and to a New York publisher placing a classified ad in the Sunday **Tribune Book World**, it may be a trade/professional journal. Yet for the first three the rates-per-line would be identical. Such factors have their effects on the averages in each category, and the charts should be read with this in mind.

GENERAL MANAGER
$80,000

Average Dollar Amounts

	Nat'l	0	1	2	3	4	5	6	7	8	9
Employment Agency Fees	16,000	17,000	++	++	++	++	24,000	16,000	20,000	++	11,650
Executive Search Firm Fees	21,200	21,800	24,000	20,000	22,000	27,400	24,000	23,750	21,600	15,200	18,000
Referral Awards	1,250	++	++	2,500	++	++	++	++	++	2,900	1,000
Advertising:											
Local	1,600	2,100	1,750	650	1,500	1,200	650	1,100	2,150	500	1,750
Regional	1,750	2,250	2,500	1,100	1,500	800	800	3,000	++	++	1,000
National	1,950	1,600	2,450	500	1,500	++	2,500	2,200	3,500	++	1,350
Trade/Professional	1,600	3,000	2,050	350	1,650	1,000	650	1,500	++	1,250	1,350
T, L & E											
Candidate	2,450	3,050	2,450	550	1,500	++	2,500	2,200	3,500	++	1,550
Recruiter	1,300	1,500	++	++	800	750	350	2,350	3,450	++	750
Relocation (Maximum)	23,200	20,650	25,000	22,500	25,000	30,000	++	19,250	28,000	8,350	34,350

0 -- New England; 1 -- North Atlantic; 2 -- Mid Atlantic; 3 -- South;
4 -- Midwest; 5 -- North Central; 6 -- Mid Central; 7 -- South Central;
8 -- Rocky Mountain; 9 -- Pacific

All figures rounded to nearest $50.

++ Insufficient sample

Table 27

GENERAL MANAGER, responsible for all aspects of product line from materials procurement to sales/marketing; reports directly to Executive V.P./COO. Minimum 18 years experience in managerial position, 8 years in senior management. Salary range: $80,000+.

Fees: Most respondents opt for search firms rather than agencies for this post, although the former typically charge 30 per cent of salary against the latter's 20 per cent. West Coast averages are significantly lower than East Coast in our sample, and Mountain States lowest of all.

Awards: Where budgeted, they are substantial. For no other position do they average as much as $500; for the general manager post, the average is more than twice that amount.

Advertising: New England and the North Atlantic region buy more space and pay more for it. Local and regional rates are importantly lower in the Mid Atlantic and South, and climb again in the Central region. Those Central areas budget more dollars in national advertising, while both Coasts figure to reach sufficient candidates locally. The South spends above the national average in trade and professional journals.

Travel, Lodging and Entertainment: Although the sample is small, Mid and South Central respondents show a greater willingness to send recruiters on the road, budgeting as much or more in that area as for candidate T, L & E. The tendency is confirmed in figures for other high-salaried posts. Where the recruiter wishes to look beyond locally available candidates, it may be more cost effective to send the recruiter out than to bring candidates in -- especially where air travel is lengthy and expensive.

Relocation: Save in the Mountain States, the figures reveal a willingness to spend what's necessary in this area.

Labor Cost/Hire: Large company costs are dramatically higher, pushed up by a low concurrent case load and a high estimate of weeks necessary to fill the position. In no other case are large company costs so far above the others. Turnover rates show little effect.

GENERAL MANAGER	Total Sample	Annual Sales			Turnover Rate	
		+$500M	$50M to $500M	-$50M	+15%	-5%
Recruiter's Annual Salary	$38,410	$38,000	$35,730	$39,740	$40,160	$33,430
Concurrent Case Load	13.9	11.2	15.9	13.5	13.7	12.4
Weeks to Fill Position	10.0	11.4	9.5	10.0	9.6	10.8
Labor Cost/Hire	$532	$744	$410	$566	$541	$559

Table 28

SENIOR FINANCIAL OFFICER
$65,000

Average Dollar Amounts

	Nat'l	0	1	2	3	4	5	6	7	8	9
Employment Agency Fees	10,400	11,300	9,250	++	7,600	13,000	17,350	9,950	8,250	++	13,700
Executive Search Firm Fees	18,050	19,000	18,200	++	19,200	17,650	17,250	18,200	16,250	17,050	18,300
Referral Awards	350	500	++	++	150	250	++	350	450	300	350
Advertising:											
Local	1,150	1,250	1,250	450	500	600	700	2,000	1,050	300	1,500
Regional	1,400	1,500	2,750	350	750	1,200	650	1,600	750	500	1,350
National	2,050	3,750	1,900	++	3,000	2,050	1,450	1,900	1,600	1,750	1,100
Trade/Professional	1,300	1,150	1,250	300	2,050	600	1,000	2,100	450	1,000	1,900
T, L & E											
Candidate	1,750	1,300	1,600	500	2,100	2,500	1,750	1,900	1,850	1,600	1,450
Recruiter	950	900	550	500	900	1,200	450	850	1,000	650	1,720
Relocation (Maximum)	15,150	14,950	15,000	++	20,150	26,400	10,150	10,650	15,650	12,350	14,800

0 -- New England; 1 -- North Atlantic; 2 -- Mid Atlantic; 3 -- South;
4 -- Midwest; 5 -- North Central; 6 -- Mid Central; 7 -- South Central;
8 -- Rocky Mountain; 9 -- Pacific

All figures rounded to nearest $50.

++ Insufficient sample

Table 29

HIRING COSTS AND STRATEGIES: THE AMA REPORT

SENIOR FINANCIAL OFFICER, responsible for financing, budgeting and related activities; master's degree in accounting or business administration; minimum 10 years experience. Salary range: $60-65,000.

Fees: Save in the North Central region, search firm fees are appreciably higher than agency charges -- in some cases, double the amount or more. Also, agency fees vary widely -- 30 per cent up and down from the national average -- while search firm fees are more uniform coast to coast.

Awards: Apparently, it's not the done thing on the Atlantic Coast from New York to South Carolina. The amounts are higher in New England and on the West Coast than in the South and Midwest/Central regions. The amounts are fairly representative for all positions over $30,000 in salary.

Advertising: As compared with other positions, respondents place greater emphasis on trade and professional advertising, especially in the South and North Central regions. National advertising levels are high across the board. Budget amounts drop in the Mid Atlantic region, which includes D.C.

Travel, Lodging and Entertainment: Save for the West Coast, a typical proportion of candidate to recruiter expenses for positions at this salary.

Relocation: In part, relocation budgets reflect the locally available talent pool. Anticipated costs in New England, the North Atlantic and the West Coast are below the national average, perhaps for that reason; the South and Midwest are above it.

Labor Cost/Hire: While paying the recruiter considerably more, large companies gain advantage with a higher concurrent case load -- a typical example.

SENIOR FINANCIAL OFFICER	Total Sample	Annual Sales			Turnover Rate	
		+$500M	$50M to $500M	-$50M	+15%	-5%
Recruiter's Annual Salary	$37,650	$41,900	$39,180	$33,430	$38,900	$38,110
Concurrent Case Load	13.4	16.2	13.2	12.1	13.5	12.8
Weeks to Fill Position	9.9	10.5	10.5	9.4	10.2	10.3
Labor Cost/Hire	$535	$522	$599	$499	$565	$589

Table 30

MIS DIRECTOR
$60,000

	Nat'l	0	1	2	3	4	5	6	7	8	9
Employment Agency Fees	12,200	11,650	12,300	10,950	13,200	16,500	18,000	16,200	6,700	9,000	9,300
Executive Search Firm Fees	15,850	15,400	15,950	16,000	17,800	17,000	17,500	16,850	13,250	9,000	16,650
Referral Awards	300	550	150	++	++	++	100	1,250	200	++	++
Advertising:											
Local	905	900	1,000	400	400	700	650	1,700	700	550	1,250
Regional	1,400	1,600	2,050	650	1,050	750	650	1,850	1,250	700	1,500
National	1,750	2,350	2,200	550	800	1,150	1,250	3,650	++	++	2,400
Trade/Professional	1,100	1,550	1,400	400	400	650	650	1,750	950	900	1,400
T, L & E											
Candidate	1,550	1,100	1,550	900	2500	1150	1350	1300	1600	1900	1800
Recruiter	500	200	400	100	600	300	200	750	400	400	900
Relocation (Maximum)	13,500	++	10,000	9,000	19,750	++	17,850	14,350	17,000	16,600	12,900

Average Dollar Amounts

0 -- New England; 1 -- North Atlantic; 2 -- Mid Atlantic; 3 -- South;
4 -- Midwest; 5 -- North Central; 6 -- Mid Central; 7 -- South Central;
8 -- Rocky Mountain; 9 -- Pacific

All figures rounded to nearest $50.

++ Insufficient sample

Table 31

HIRING COSTS AND STRATEGIES: THE AMA REPORT

MIS DIRECTOR, responsible for systems programming, telecommunications, hardware and software evaluation and purchasing; budgetary responsibilities, capacity planning. Minimum 10 years experience; advanced degree in computer sciences or related field. Salary range: $55-60,000.

Fees: The gap between agency and search firm fees narrows for this position, especially in the South and Central sections, where the figures are nearly identical. On either Coast, the relative fees are more in agreement with earlier examples.

Awards: Not an especially popular option; half the areas show insufficient samples. A high-ticket item in the Mid Central region.

Advertising: Lots of national advertising dollars outside the South and Rocky Mountains. Low local costs outside New York, Chicago and Los Angeles.

Travel, Lodging and Entertainment: Very representative figures, not only in terms of actual cost but also in relative expenditures on candidates and recruiters.

Relocation: Insufficient samples in New England and Midwest reveal an expectation of filling the position locally. Budgets in the North Atlantic and West Coast regions, lower than national average, reflect the same attitude.

Labor Cost/Hire: An especially high case load among large company respondents push costs below others. Low turnover companies expect to fill the post in significantly less time than high-turnover firms.

MIS DIRECTOR	Total Sample	Annual Sales			Turnover Rate	
		+$500M	$50M to $500M	-$50M	+15%	-5%
Recruiter's Annual Salary	$34,320	$38,700	$33,190	$32,980	$36,050	$31,830
Concurrent Case Load	16.1	20.3	15.3	13.2	16.4	16.9
Weeks to Fill Position	9.8	9.6	11.2	8.6	10.5	8.8
Labor Cost/Hire	$400	$352	$467	$413	$444	$319

Table 32

PURCHASING DIRECTOR
$50,000

Average Dollar Amounts

	Nat'l	0	1	2	3	4	5	6	7	8	9
Employment Agency Fees	8,000	++	10,150	++	10,000	10,250	8,150	5,750	7,500	++	12,500
Executive Search Firm Fees	12,150	15,000	11,900	5,000	++	15,400	13,350	13,750	7,500	++	++
Referral Awards	200	300	++	++	++	++	++	++	++	++	650
Advertising:											
Local	900	700	400	++	++	500	900	200	350	++	1,450
Regional	1,350	++	1,500	++	900	1,550	1,500	1,750	400	++	2,000
National	1,950	++	2,750	++	++	650	3,000	++	++	++	1,850
Trade/Professional	700	650	++	++	300	500	++	2,000	650	++	1,000
T, L & E											
Candidate	1,150	1,050	1,600	600	650	600	2,000	2,050	2,500	++	++
Recruiter	400	++	650	50	++	200	650	100	++	++	400
Relocation (Maximum)	7,000	15,000	5,000	++	++	6,650	++	++	++	++	25,000

0 -- New England;   1 -- North Atlantic;   2 -- Mid Atlantic;   3 -- South;
4 -- Midwest;   5 -- North Central;   6 -- Mid Central;   7 -- South Central;
8 -- Rocky Mountain;   9 -- Pacific

All figures rounded to nearest $50.

++ Insufficient sample

Table 33

HIRING COSTS AND STRATEGIES: THE AMA REPORT

DIRECTOR OF PURCHASING, responsible for implementing new inventory procedures, inventory reduction, vendor relations, coordination with manufacturing and marketing departments; MBA or similar degree; minimum 10 years experience. Salary range: $47-50,000.

Fees: Agency charges here are generally two-thirds those of search firms, but respondents are equally likely to chose the one as the other. South Central respondents report no difference in fees.

Awards: Hardly a popular strategy for this position.

Advertising: Respondents report very individualistic patterns: heavy national advertising among North Atlantic and North Central respondents, none at all in six other regions. West Coast firms report high advertising expenditures in all media.

Travel, Lodging and Entertainment: Monies allocated to candidate T, L & E are quite high in the Central regions, low or nonexistent elsewhere. The budgets for recruiter expenses align with the averages for all positions.

Relocation: Very low amounts where budgeted at all, save on the West Coast.

Labor Cost/Hire: The high cost reported by low-turnover companies is due to the expectation factor. Their average of 9.6 weeks to fill the position is 30 per cent higher than the national average.

PURCHASING DIRECTOR	Total Sample	Annual Sales			Turnover Rate	
		+$500M	$50M to $500M	-$50M	+15%	-5%
Recruiter's Annual Salary	$33,710	$43,170	$35,170	$29,440	$35,190	$31,800
Concurrent Case Load	14.8	23.1	14.8	11.6	14.6	10.0
Weeks to Fill Position	7.3	7.4	8.9	5.9	6.8	9.6
Labor Cost/Hire	$321	$320	$407	$287	$315	$587

Table 34

SALES MANAGER
$45,000

Average Dollar Amounts

	Nat'l	0	1	2	3	4	5	6	7	8	9
Employment Agency Fees	6,950	7,100	4,600	++	4,500	++	5,400	8,550	3,300	++	9,550
Executive Search Firm Fees	10,950	13,050	12,150	4,500	7,500	13,300	9,300	10,150	11,250	13,500	11,550
Referral Awards	300	300	200	++	++	500	100	500	200	250	400
Advertising:											
Local	1,350	1,000	1,050	++	650	1,700	1,050	1,950	700	++	2,200
Regional	1,450	1,350	2,000	++	1,000	1,600	1,250	700	600	++	2,150
National	1,850	2,100	2,150	++	2,650	1,300	3,000	1,250	650	++	1,850
Trade/Professional	1,050	1,320	800	++	1,750	450	3,750	750	550	++	500
T, L & E											
Candidate	1,550	1,100	1,400	++	1,500	1,050	2,400	1,550	2,750	++	1,400
Recruiter	1,100	850	800	++	1,150	650	1,300	2,350	1,300	++	1,500
Relocation (Maximum)	11,500	7,650	20,000	++	7,350	21,500	4,000	8,000	++	++	++

0 -- New England; 1 -- North Atlantic; 2 -- Mid Atlantic; 3 -- South;
4 -- Midwest; 5 -- North Central; 6 -- Mid Central; 7 -- South Central;
8 -- Rocky Mountain; 9 -- Pacific

All figures rounded to nearest $50.

++ Insufficient sample

Table 35

SALES MANAGER, responsible for directing national sales force, determining staff needs, evaluating distribution channels, developing accounts and forecasting sales. BA in business, marketing, or related field; minimum 5 years sales experience, 3 years management experience. Salary range: $42-45,000, plus performance bonus.

Fees: The range for agency fees runs from ten per cent in the South to just over 20 per cent on the West Coast, with a national average of 15 per cent. Save in the South, search firm charges begin where agency fees end, and are upwards of 30 per cent in New England and the Midwest.

Awards: A standard practice outside the South, and the amounts are fairly standard as well.

Advertising: Relatively high local expenditures are reported for this position, and spending in all categories is above the norm, not just for all positions but also for posts at this salary level. This restates the findings in Section I: that recruitment costs for sales managers are out of proportion to the salary.

Travel, Lodging and Entertainment: Again, expenses are unusually high, reflecting the premium placed on filling this vital position.

Relocation: The relatively low budgets in this category do not reflect the large number of respondents who place no maximum and would spend "whatever it takes" to sign the preferred candidate.

Labor Cost/Hire: Again, a remarkably high case load for large companies -- more than double the figure for small firms -- lowers the cost.

SALES MANAGER	Total Sample	Annual Sales			Turnover Rate	
		+$500M	$50M to $500M	-$50M	+15%	-5%
Recruiter's Annual Salary	$35,760	$36,360	$38,710	$32,430	$37,750	$38,000
Concurrent Case Load	16.0	27.1	16.5	12.4	15.1	16.1
Weeks to Fill Position	8.6	9.9	7.3	8.4	9.1	7.9
Labor Cost/Hire	$370	$255	$329	$422	$437	$359

Table 36

PLANT PERSONNEL MANAGER

$42,000

Average Dollar Amounts

	Nat'l	0	1	2	3	4	5	6	7	8	9
Employment Agency Fees	6,500	6,150	10,150	++	3,500	6,050	6,500	5,950	6,500	2,300	4,350
Executive Search Firm Fees	11,700	11,650	10,900	++	12,600	13,300	10,500	12,850	9,650	11,550	15,750
Referral Awards	350	500	++	++	150	++	++	300	300	++	1,000
Advertising:											
Local	650	800	750	600	500	550	650	1,200	600	150	550
Regional	1,100	800	1,150	200	500	1,300	650	1,400	1,150	500	1,250
National	1,650	1,650	2,350	++	2,000	++	2,000	1,750	2,000	1,000	1,000
Trade/Professional	1,000	++	500	100	1,900	750	700	1,750	650	800	650
T, L & E											
Candidate	1,300	1,000	1,700	450	1,300	1,900	1,150	1,850	1,150	1,000	950
Recruiter	550	300	450	100	500	550	150	100	50	750	200
Relocation (Maximum)	15,150	13,600	16,200	3,500	22,500	10,800	20,000	20,000	19,750	25,000	17,450

0 -- New England; 1 -- North Atlantic; 2 -- Mid Atlantic; 3 -- South;
4 -- Midwest; 5 -- North Central; 6 -- Mid Central; 7 -- South Central;
8 -- Rocky Mountain; 9 -- Pacific

All figures rounded to nearest $50.

++ Insufficient sample

Table 37

PLANT PERSONNEL MANAGER, responsible for labor relations, EEO compliance, training and development for all aspects of manufacturing operations. Degree in labor/industrial relations or plant management; minimum 5 to 7 years experience. Salary range: $40-42,000.

Fees: Agency fees top out at 15 per cent of annual salary, save for the aberrational figure in the North Atlantic region. For search firms the national average is close to 30 per cent, and tops one-third of the annual salary on the West Coast.

Awards: Again, West Coast budgets are significantly higher here, while fewer than half the regions provide any budgets at all in this category.

Advertising: Highest expenditures across the board are reported in the Mid Central region, which includes Illinois and Missouri. Conversely, extremely low budgets for this post show in the service economies of District of Columbia and environs.

Travel, Lodging and Entertainment: The industrial Midwest and Mid Central regions budget above the national average to fill this industrial position.

Relocation: High figures are reported across the board, even in the South, which usually trails the national averages in this category.

Labor Cost/Hire: The range between high-turnover and low-turnover companies is due to the latter's lesser case load and higher recruiter salary.

PLANT PERSONNEL MGR.	Total Sample	Annual Sales			Turnover Rate	
		+$500M	$50M to $500M	-$50M	+15%	-5%
Recruiter's Annual Salary	$34,330	$38,100	$35,780	$30,300	$32,570	$37,380
Concurrent Case Load	13.7	14.5	13.5	13.1	14.8	10.0
Weeks to Fill Position	7.7	8.0	8.4	7.0	8.0	8.9
Labor Cost/Hire	$371	$404	$428	$311	$339	$640

Table 38

PRODUCT MANAGER
$38,000

Average Dollar Amounts

	Nat'l	0	1	2	3	4	5	6	7	8	9
Employment Agency Fees	7,900	7,500	7,050	5,700	5,050	10,750	9,500	10,650	7,100	7,600	8,100
Executive Search Firm Fees	8,800	8,100	10,150	++	8,550	9,500	++	10,650	8,250	7,600	8,250
Referral Awards	350	150	350	++	++	++	++	++	1,000	2,000	500
Advertising:											
Local	1,000	1,150	1,250	2,000	450	650	300	800	900	450	1,850
Regional	1,700	1,700	2,850	300	1,250	1,750	200	1,700	2,350	1,500	2,250
National	1,300	650	++	200	1,000	++	++	2,200	++	1,000	++
Trade/Professional	950	1,000	++	250	650	1,150	200	750	++	300	1,000
T, L & E											
Candidate	1,450	1,200	1,450	550	1,600	1,850	1,050	2,350	1,150	850	2,200
Recruiter	550	++	350	++	550	700	500	850	800	++	750
Relocation (Maximum)	11,950	9,000	12,000	5,000	4,000	18,000	15,000	17,650	8,250	7,000	21,750

0 -- New England; 1 -- North Atlantic; 2 -- Mid Atlantic; 3 -- South;
4 -- Midwest; 5 -- North Central; 6 -- Mid Central; 7 -- South Central;
8 -- Rocky Mountain; 9 -- Pacific

All figures rounded to nearest $50.

++ Insufficient sample

Table 39

HIRING COSTS AND STRATEGIES: THE AMA REPORT

PRODUCT MANAGER, responsible for supervision of production line work teams, quality control, work assignments; degree in engineering or related field; minimum 8 years experience. Salary range: $35-38,000.

<u>Fees</u>: As the salary level drops below $40,000, the difference between agency and search firm fees narrows or disappears. Here, the national average for agencies is 21 per cent of annual salary; for search firms, 23 per cent. This similarity continues through the remainder of the position charts.

<u>Awards</u>: Unusually high figures are found on the South Central and Rocky Mountain regions, but the samples border on insufficiency.

<u>Advertising</u>: Uncharacteristically high budgets for local advertising along both the Atlantic and Pacific Coasts; regional costs are high in the middle of the country. National advertising budgets begin to drop for this position; only half the regions report a sufficient sample.

<u>Travel, Lodging and Entertainment</u>: The figures are very close to the national standard, both in amounts relative to salary and in ratios between candidate and recruiter budgets.

<u>Relocation</u>: Again, very much the standard breakdown: low budgets in the South and the Rockies, proportionally higher costs on the West Coast.

<u>Labor Cost/Hire</u>: Again, the comparative figures are typical: large companies gain the advantage with a concurrent case load more than double the number for small firms.

PRODUCT MANAGER	Total Sample	Annual Sales			Turnover Rate	
		+$500M	$50M to $500M	-$50M	+15%	-5%
Recruiter's Annual Salary	$33,190	$37,830	$29,360	$34,660	$32,430	29,670
Concurrent Case Load	15.4	25.2	16.3	11.5	15.9	14.9
Weeks to Fill Position	7.5	7.2	8.5	7.0	8.1	7.1
Labor Cost/Hire	$311	$208	$294	$406	$318	$272

Table 40

Average Dollar Amounts

MARKET RESEARCH MGR. $35,000	Nat'l	0	1	2	3	4	5	6	7	8	9
Employment Agency Fees	6,700	5,950	8,250	8,150	5,850	7,000	8,750	5,250	++	3,500	4,400
Executive Search Firm Fees	8,250	7,350	7,000	++	++	9,350	8,750	9,650	++	5,250	8,150
Referral Awards	350	300	++	1,000	++	++	200	350	++	++	++
Advertising:											
Local	800	1,100	450	500	700	700	600	1,500	950	550	1,000
Regional	1,100	++	1,450	1,250	++	650	700	1,350	1,200	++	++
National	1,100	++	1,400	400	200	800	500	700	++	++	2,000
Trade/Professional	850	1,500	550	300	500	750	100	850	500	++	1,450
T, L & E											
Candidate	1,050	1,100	2,050	850	1,650	800	700	150	250	1,000	1,100
Recruiter	300	++	300	350	++	500	200	150	50	500	750
Relocation (Maximum)	11,400	9,350	10,000	13,350	11,500	++	10,350	17,500	11,500	22,500	10,450

0 -- New England; 1 -- North Atlantic; 2 -- Mid Atlantic; 3 -- South;
4 -- Midwest; 5 -- North Central; 6 -- Mid Central; 7 -- South Central;
8 -- Rocky Mountain; 9 -- Pacific

All figures rounded to nearest $50.

++ Insufficient sample

Table 41

MARKET RESEARCH MANAGER, responsible for supervising and analyzing research projects for existing and new products and services, designing research instruments, conducting field work and focus groups. Degree (MBA preferred); 3 to 5 years experience. Salary range: $32-35,000.

Fees: Agency charges show a wide range for this position, from a high of 25 per cent on the Atlantic Coast to 10 per cent in the Rockies. Search firm fees are high in the Midwest and Central regions, and again low in the Rocky Mountains. A small sample accounts for the unusually high figure reported in the South.

Awards: Only four of the ten regions report a sufficient sample, and the national figure is skewed by the uncharacteristically high number in the Mid Atlantic region.

Advertising: Choices here and in the positions that follow become more individualistic and less subject to generalization. Nevertheless, the study's overall finding of high costs on either Coast and lower rates in the South and the Mountains continues to hold true.

Travel, Lodging and Entertainment: At these salary levels the budgeted amounts begin to shrink, especially for recruiter expenses. Again the South's average is high due to a small sample.

Relocation: This is the last position for which the national average tops $10,000. Relative costs also become less representative, due to a falling number of respondents in all regions who report expenditures in this category.

Labor Cost/Hire: Here too, costs diminish and the range among sample categories becomes less severe. Large companies retain their advantage with higher case loads per recruiter, offsetting salaries which are generally 20 per cent higher.

MARKET RESEARCH MGR.	Total Sample	Annual Sales +$500M	$50M to $500M	-$50M	Turnover Rate +15%	-5%
Recruiter's Annual Salary	$31,450	$34,640	$31,900	$28,860	$31,810	$29,860
Concurrent Case Load	14.2	17.1	16.5	11.5	16.8	15.3
Weeks to Fill Position	7.9	8.0	8.5	7.3	7.9	8.7
Labor Cost/Hire	$326	$312	$316	$352	$288	$327

Table 42

TELEMARKETING MANAGER
$32,000

Average Dollar Amounts

	Nat'l	0	1	2	3	4	5	6	7	8	9
Employment Agency Fees	6,100	4,950	6,400	++	++	++	++	8,000	++	3,200	7,450
Executive Search Firm Fees	7,100	6,400	6,950	++	++	++	++	5,600	++	8,000	8,000
Referral Awards	400	500	++	++	++	++	++	400	++	++	550
Advertising:											
Local	1,450	1,200	1,000	++	++	++	900	1,350	++	300	2,150
Regional	1,400	1,500	++	++	++	++	++	++	++	500	1,650
National	++	++	1,200	++	++	++	700	++	++	800	1,000
Trade/Professional	950	1,000	++	++	++	++	700	++	++	800	1,000
T, L & E											
Candidate	950	500	++	++	++	++	1,000	500	++	1,500	1,150
Recruiter	500	150	100	++	++	++	100	750	++	1,150	++
Relocation (Maximum)	4,100	++	2,500	++	++	++	++	++	++	12,000	++

0 -- New England; 1 -- North Atlantic; 2 -- Mid Atlantic; 3 -- South;
4 -- Midwest; 5 -- North Central; 6 -- Mid Central; 7 -- South Central;
8 -- Rocky Mountain; 9 -- Pacific

All figures rounded to nearest $50.

++ Insufficient sample

Table 43

TELEMARKETING MANAGER, responsible for design and direction of new telemarketing operation; recruiting, training and supervising staff, selecting target lists, developing phone scripts. Minimum 5 years experience in telemarketing; management experience preferred but not essential. Salary range: $30-32,000.

Fees: The small national sample for this position naturally breaks down into even smaller regional samples, to the point where half the regions give too few numbers for valid entries. Still, the national figures are in keeping with our findings for other positions at this salary level. Agency and search firm fees are similar, topping out at 25 per cent in the Mid Central region (for agencies) and in the Mountains and West Coast (for search firms).

Awards: Where budgeted, the numbers are comparatively high for a position at this salary.

Advertising: Scattered findings, but the pattern holds: high local costs on both coasts and in Illinois.

Travel, Lodging and Entertainment: The ranges and samples reflect how new the position is; too soon for a national consensus to form.

Relocation: The sample is too spotty for conclusions to be drawn.

Labor Cost/Hire: The national average of 9.6 weeks to fill the post is extraordinarily high for a position at this salary, and again reflects the lack of experience in finding candidates with these qualifications.

TELEMARKETING MANAGER	Total Sample	Annual Sales			Turnover Rate	
		+$500M	$50M to $500M	-$50M	+15%	-5%
Recruiter's Annual Salary	$28,720	$33,750	$29,830	$24,570	$27,310	$30,000
Concurrent Case Load	12.6	16.3	11.6	11.2	12.2	10.0
Weeks to Fill Position	9.6	9.2	8.3	11.3	11.2	5.5
Labor Cost/Hire	$421	$366	$410	$477	$482	$317

Table 44

COMPUTER PROGRAMMER
$28,000

Average Dollar Amounts

	Nat'l	0	1	2	3	4	5	6	7	8	9
Employment Agency Fees	4,550	4,450	4,800	6,300	3,100	5,500	5,100	4,700	3,500	2,800	5,250
Executive Search Firm Fees	6,650	++	7,000	++	++	7,550	5,600	8,400	5,600	++	6,650
Referral Awards	450	900	1,000	++	300	350	150	300	150	300	400
Advertising:											
Local	800	900	700	400	500	1,100	800	1,200	550	100	800
Regional	950	1,100	1,000	1,000	800	950	1,400	1,100	650	++	1,000
National	1,550	++	1,100	++	1,500	2,750	++	++	++	++	++
Trade/Professional	1,000	750	1,500	++	1,350	850	++	200	650	100	1,000
T, L & E											
Candidate	650	400	450	300	1,350	950	850	600	100	550	400
Recruiter	400	350	50	++	850	650	350	100	100	++	700
Relocation (Maximum)	8,900	11,200	6,000	10,000	12,650	6,200	7,000	++	2,000	3,000	16,200

0 -- New England; 1 -- North Atlantic; 2 -- Mid Atlantic; 3 -- South;
4 -- Midwest; 5 -- North Central; 6 -- Mid Central; 7 -- South Central;
8 -- Rocky Mountain; 9 -- Pacific

All figures rounded to nearest $50.

++ Insufficient sample

Table 45

HIRING COSTS AND STRATEGIES: THE AMA REPORT

COMPUTER PROGRAMMER, to aid in developing special applications mainframe software and training staff in use thereof; degree in computer sciences or related field; entry level; hands-on mainframe experience required. Salary range: $26-28,000.

Fees: For this entry-level position, agency fees average 16.5 per cent nationally, and are lowest in the South (11 per cent), highest in the Mid Atlantic region (22.5 per cent) and on the West Coast (18.8 per cent). Search firm fees are 50 per cent higher or more, but far fewer respondents would use them for this post.

Awards: The strategy is unusually popular for this position, and the figures highest on the Atlantic coast; elsewhere the amounts are more typical of awards at this salary level.

Advertising: Most respondents believe they can fill this post through local or regional advertising. Only three regions yield sufficient samples for national ad budgets, and those figures vary widely.

Travel, Lodging and Entertainment: The figures for the South, Midwest, and North Central regions raise the national average considerably; elsewhere the T, L & E budgets for this post are not high, and for recruiters are quite low.

Relocation: The figures should be read in light of the fact that two-thirds of our respondents would budget no monies at all for relocation expenses for this position.

Labor Cost/Hire: The low costs are a reflection of the speed with which most respondents expect to fill the post.

COMPUTER PROGRAMMER	Total Sample	Annual Sales			Turnover Rate	
		+$500M	$50M to $500M	-$50M	+15%	-5%
Recruiter's Annual Salary	$31,150	$34,470	$29,860	$30,480	$30,930	$32,470
Concurrent Case Load	16.0	20.6	16.7	13.2	16.0	13.4
Weeks to Fill Position	6.3	6.7	6.6	5.8	6.9	6.3
Labor Cost/Hire	$235	$215	$227	$258	$257	$294

Table 46

HUMAN RESOURCES SPEC.
$28,000

Average Dollar Amounts

	Nat'l	0	1	2	3	4	5	6	7	8	9
Employment Agency Fees	5,450	5,050	5,000	2,800	6,500	4,900	++	6,100	4,650	++	6,150
Executive Search Firm Fees	5,450	5,000	4,650	++	8,400	5,600	++	7,000	3,900	++	5,300
Referral Awards	250	250	250	500	++	150	200	250	250	++	150
Advertising:											
Local	700	600	600	550	500	750	400	1,250	350	500	900
Regional	1,000	1,050	850	200	1,000	850	700	1,220	850	600	1,800
National	1,150	1,400	1,000	500	950	500	++	++	++	300	++
Trade/Professional	500	200	350	250	950	750	100	750	900	300	++
T, L & E											
Candidate	800	500	550	600	1,600	700	400	1,050	750	1,050	600
Recruiter	450	++	100	300	750	700	++	750	650	150	400
Relocation (Maximum)	8,250	++	5,350	16,650	2,000	12,350	5,000	12,000	3,350	11,500	5,800

0 -- New England; 1 -- North Atlantic; 2 -- Mid Atlantic; 3 -- South;
4 -- Midwest; 5 -- North Central; 6 -- Mid Central; 7 -- South Central;
8 -- Rocky Mountain; 9 -- Pacific

Table 47

All figures rounded to nearest $50.

++ Insufficient sample

HIRING COSTS AND STRATEGIES: THE AMA REPORT

HUMAN RESOURCES SPECIALIST, responsible for recruitment, job placement, career counseling and group counseling. Minimum 2-3 years experience; master's degree in personnel or related field. Salary range: $26-28,000.

Fees: At this salary level, the national figures for agency and search firm fees are identical: just under 20 per cent of annual salary. As reported in Section 1, twice as many respondents would opt for agencies over search firms to fill this spot, and a majority would use neither.

Awards: The amounts are typical for the salary level.

Advertising: As with all posts under the $30,000 level, the dollars are spent primarily on local and regional ad space, and the actual dollar amounts are not high.

Travel, Lodging and Entertainment: The amounts are scaled more toward bringing candidates cross-town than cross-country, but proportionally the numbers for recruiter expenses are high, save on the Atlantic Coast.

Relocation: Again, bear in mind that less than 20 per cent of all respondents would budget more than $5,000 for relocation costs for this position, and 55 per cent would pay nothing at all.

Labor Cost/Hire: An example of how the variables even out: despite different recruiter salaries, case loads, and hiring expectations, the LC/H is identical for large, mid-sized and small firms.

HUMAN RESOURCES SPEC.	Total Sample	Annual Sales			Turnover Rate	
		+$500M	$50M to $500M	-$50M	+15%	-5%
Recruiter's Annual Salary	$31,280	$33,410	$29,520	$32,450	$31,520	$28,670
Concurrent Case Load	15.2	17.5	14.6	13.4	16.2	15.0
Weeks to Fill Position	7.2	8.1	7.6	6.4	7.2	8.4
Labor Cost/Hire	$297	$297	$296	$298	$269	$309

Table 48

STAFF ACCOUNTANT
$26,000

Average Dollar Amounts

	Nat'l	0	1	2	3	4	5	6	7	8	9
Employment Agency Fees	4,850	5,200	5,100	3,250	++	++	4,550	5,200	2,600	5,200	2,600
Executive Search Firm Fees	5,100	4,550	++	2,600	++	++	2,600	7,800	++	5,200	5,200
Referral Awards	150	400	150	++	++	++	++	++	100	++	++
Advertising:											
Local	700	850	950	150	650	500	400	650	700	100	1,150
Regional	800	++	++	100	++	350	700	400	++	200	2,000
National	300	++	++	++	++	500	++	200	++	200	++
Trade/Professional	100	200	++	150	++	++	++	650	++	++	++
T, L & E											
Candidate	300	200	650	100	100	200	300	++	250	200	500
Recruiter	100	50	150	++	++	400	100	++	++	++	300
Relocation (Maximum)	6,150	++	++	++	++	++	4,500	++	11,500	5,000	++

0 -- New England; 1 -- North Atlantic; 2 -- Mid Atlantic; 3 -- South;
4 -- Midwest; 5 -- North Central; 6 -- Mid Central; 7 -- South Central;
8 -- Rocky Mountain; 9 -- Pacific

All figures rounded to nearest $50.

++ Insufficient sample

Table 49

STAFF ACCOUNTANT, responsible for monthly closings, journal entry preparation, account analysis and statement preparation, occasional special project assignments. Master's degree in accounting; some experience preferred but not essential (possible entry-level position). Salary range: $24-26,000.

<u>Fees</u>: Section I discussed how inexact are the definitions which separate an employment agency from an executive search firm. The problem is especially pronounced at the low end of the salary scale for positions outlined in this report. The differences in dollar amounts have more to do with this problem of definition than with regional factors.

<u>Awards</u>: Not many respondents offer them, and the amounts are not high.

<u>Advertising</u>: For most respondents, local advertising is entirely sufficient to fill this post. The national expenditures are practically non-existent.

<u>Travel, Lodging and Entertainment</u>: Not a significant expense for either candidates or recruiters.

<u>Relocation</u>: Once more, the sample is miniscule.

<u>Labor Cost/Hire</u>: The lowest for any position, due to the swiftness with which the position can be filled.

STAFF ACCOUNTANT	Total Sample	Annual Sales			Turnover Rate	
		+$500M	$50M to $500M	-$50M	+15%	-5%
Recruiter's Annual Salary	$31,370	$36,550	$31,410	$29,540	$30,220	$29,880
Concurrent Case Load	14.8	18.5	15.8	12.6	14.6	10.0
Weeks to Fill Position	5.5	6.2	5.2	5.7	5.8	6.0
Labor Cost/Hire	$224	$236	$199	$257	$231	$345

Table 50

HIRING COSTS AND STRATEGIES: THE AMA REPORT

POSTAL ZIP CODES BY STATE

Alabama -- 3	Kentucky -- 4	North Dakota -- 5
Alaska -- 9	Louisiana -- 7	Ohio -- 4
Arizona -- 8	Maine -- 0	Oklahoma -- 6
Arkansas -- 7	Maryland -- 2	Oregon -- 9
California -- 9	Massachusetts -- 0	Pennsylvania -- 1
Colorado -- 8	Michigan -- 4	Rhode Island -- 0
Connecticut -- 0	Minnesota -- 5	South Carolina -- 2
Delaware -- 2	Mississippi -- 3	South Dakota -- 5
Dist. of Columbia -- 2	Missouri -- 6	Tennessee -- 3
Florida -- 3	Montana -- 5	Texas -- 7
Georgia -- 3	Nebraska -- 6	Utah -- 8
Hawaii -- 9	Nevada -- 8	Vermont -- 0
New Hampshire -- 0	Idaho -- 8	Virginia -- 2
Illinois -- 6	New Jersey -- 1*	Washington -- 9
Indiana -- 4	New Mexico -- 8	Wisconsin -- 5
Iowa -- 5	New York -- 1	Wyoming -- 8
Kansas -- 6	North Carolina -- 2	

* Although New Jersey ZIP codes begin with 0, figures from respondents in New Jersey have been grouped with New York and Pennsylvania (1).

SECTION III

THE RESPONDENT PROFILE

Four hundred and fifty respondents returned usable questionnaires. Not all answered every question or chose three position descriptions on which to base their answers. This resulted in 1,198 usable responses spread among the twelve position descriptions on the questionnaire's two forms.

The questionnaire's first page asked for information on organization size, location, economic activity and management turnover rates. The tables in this section are compilations of that data.

RESPONDENTS BY ECONOMIC ACTIVITY

	Total Sample	Annual Sales			Turnover Rate	
		+$500M	$50M to $500M	-$50M	+15%	-5%
Diversified Conglomorate	11	4	2	5	7	0
Banking/Finance	29	8	7	6	15	4
Communications/Publishing	13	2	5	5	9	1
Construction	5	1	0	4	3	1
Education	24	2	8	13	14	4
Entertainment/Recreation/Lodging	7	1	4	2	5	0
Food Processing/Agribusiness	12	3	7	2	5	3
Government/Military	38	8	10	18	14	2
Health Care/Medical	38	2	13	22	19	4
Insurance	19	4	7	8	11	3
Manufacturing: Consumer Goods	40	6	13	20	20	5
Manufacturing: Industrial Goods	85	13	32	37	34	13
Mineral Extraction/Processing	8	2	3	3	3	1
Professional Services	24	0	4	20	13	4
Trade (Wholesale/Retail)	16	8	3	4	14	1
Transportation/Distribution	13	6	6	1	6	1
Utilities	11	6	4	1	2	3
Other	55	5	14	36	26	13

Table 51

HIRING COSTS AND STRATEGIES: THE AMA REPORT

RESPONDENTS BY GEOGRAPHIC DISTRIBUTION/ORGANIZATIONAL SIZE

		Total Sample	+$500M	Annual Sales $50M to $500M	-$50M
0	New England	66	13	20	33
1	North Atlantic	60	16	19	25
2	Mid Atlantic	25	1	10	14
3	South	31	10	8	13
4	Midwest	51	9	15	27
5	North Central	35	8	13	14
6	Mid Central	38	8	13	17
7	South Central	33	3	11	19
8	Rocky Mountain	19	1	7	11
9	Pacific	66	13	24	29

Table 52

RESPONDENTS BY GEOGRAPHIC DISTRIBUTION/ECONOMIC ACTIVITY

	Nat'l	0	1	2	3	4	5	6	7	8	9
Diversified Conglomorate	11	0	3	0	0	1	0	1	0	2	4
Banking/Finance	29	5	5	1	3	4	0	1	2	2	6
Communications/Publishing	13	4	3	1	1	0	0	2	0	1	1
Construction	5	2	0	1	0	0	1	0	1	0	0
Education	24	2	4	3	2	2	0	1	3	0	7
Entertainment/Recreation/Lodging	7	0	1	1	2	0	0	1	0	1	1
Food Processing/Agribusiness	12	0	1	0	1	2	6	0	1	0	1
Government/Military	38	2	0	5	3	4	5	3	5	3	8
Health Care/Medical	38	10	8	2	3	4	0	3	4	2	2
Insurance	19	1	4	1	2	2	3	3	1	1	0
Manufacturing: Consumer Goods	40	7	4	1	2	10	3	6	1	0	5
Manufacturing: Industrial Goods	85	20	13	1	3	11	7	6	8	2	11
Mineral Extraction/Processing	8	0	3	0	0	0	1	1	1	1	0
Professional Services	24	3	3	2	2	3	3	4	0	1	2
Trade (Wholesale/Retail)	16	4	2	0	1	3	2	1	0	0	2
Transportation/Distribution	13	1	0	0	3	0	0	2	0	0	6
Utilities	11	2	1	1	1	0	1	0	0	1	3
Other	55	6	6	6	4	7	3	5	2	3	8

Table 53

RESPONDENTS PER POSITION DESCRIPTION BY SALES/TURNOVER RATES

	Total Sample*	Annual Sales			Turnover Rate	
		+$500M	$50M to $500M	-$50M	+15%	-5%
All Positions	1198	232	394	537	585	167
General Manager, $+80K	63	9	18	34	27	12
Senior Financial Officer, $60-$65K	156	33	44	74	76	23
MIS Director, $55-60K	132	27	50	52	69	15
Purchasing Director, $47-$50K	48	7	19	20	22	7
Sales Manager, $42-45K	88	12	23	47	41	14
Plant Personnel Manager, $40-$42K	114	26	39	46	55	17
Product Manager, $35-$38K	93	14	30	49	42	18
Market Research Manager, $32-35K	78	16	31	27	42	7
Telemarketing Manager, $30-32K	24	5	7	10	15	3
Computer Programmer, $26-28K	182	34	60	81	84	25
Human Resource Specialist, $26-$28K	120	27	43	46	59	14
Staff Accountant, $24-26K	96	12	30	51	53	12

Table 54

A large amount of data was gathered in the AMA Survey of Hiring Costs and Strategies. The database remains available for reconfiguration and study. We invite readers with further interest in the figures to contact the Project Director, Eric Rolfe Greenberg, at AMA's New York headquarters, 135 West 50th Street, New York, N.Y. 10020. A consultancy fee will be charged for computational time.